Receptivity

Receptivity

Francis Kelly Nemeck, O.M.I.

Wipf and Stock Publishers
150 West Broadway • Eugene OR 97401

Imprimi Potest: Michael Pfeifer, O.M.I.,
Provincial of the Southern United States Province

Imprimatur: + *Thomas J. Drury, Bishop of Corpus Christi, Texas*

Wipf and Stock Publishers
150 West Broadway
Eugene, Oregon 97401

Receptivity
By Nemeck, Francis Kelly
©1985 Nemeck, Francis Kelly
ISBN: 1-57910-538-6
Publication date: July, 2002
Previously published by Vantage Press, 1985.

To

Christ Jesus:
Yesterday—Today—Forever

in

Loving Memory

of

Francis Leonard "Kelly" Nemeck
(1910–1960)

"I believe that what we suffer in this life
can in no way be compared with the glory which
is awaiting us" (Rom. 8:18).

Contents

Preface

Receptivity is a study of what it means to be receptive to God as found in the spiritual theology of Père Pierre Teilhard de Chardin and compared with certain aspects of the dark night of the soul in St. John of the Cross.

Receptivity is the fundamental and all-pervasive attitude of creature vis-à-vis Creator: What have we—indeed, what are we—that we have not received? (1 Cor. 4:7). Our awareness of the quality of our receptivity attains a particularly acute degree of consciousness in suffering and in praying. Intense suffering and profound prayer are the ordinary milieus in which we experience most unmistakably our inner poverty before God, together with his incomparable love transforming us in himself.

This book then deals with the mystery of suffering and the mystery of praying as they converge deep within us to form our personal response to letting God be done within us. In a sense, therefore, this study views suffering as praying, or at least as a unique potential to pray.

General Notes to the Reader

Note 1. The research which underlies this book began originally as a doctoral study under the direction of Henri Cardinal de Lubac, S.J. Those studies led to a dissertation entitled *Les "passivités" dans la mystique teilhardienne* (1973). This was later co-published by Les Editions Desclée (Paris) and by Les Editions Bellarmin (Montreal) as volume 20 of their series *Hier/Aujourd'hui* under the title *Teilhard de Chardin et Jean de la Croix* (1975). *Receptivity* (1985) represents a completely revised presentation of the original research redacted in the light of subsequent insight and adapted to an English-speaking readership.

Note 2. References to the works of Teilhard are made to English translations whenever possible. References to the writings of St. John of the Cross are made in the usual manner. All translations of either author as well as of biblical passages in this study are my own. I frequently adapt these texts to express contemporary inclusive language.

Note 3. There are two peculiarities notable in Teilhard's literary style: (1) He often capitalizes words which ordinarily would not be capitalized either in French or in English. He does this for emphasis or to give them a special meaning. I have retained this element of his style since it does serve a useful purpose in interpreting certain passages; for example, *le Monde,* the World. (2) Teilhard coins and even "creates" many words and technical expressions particular to himself. Usually I paraphrase these into

xiii

intelligible English (e.g., *par traversée*, by going all the way through). Sometimes I transliterate them (e.g., *le Christique*, the Christic). Once in a while I retain the French word itself (e.g., *Milieu*, Milieu).

Note 4. Following the Western mystical tradition, both John and Teilhard use the word "soul" (*anima, el alma, l'âme*) as synonymous with "person," stressing the interiority of that person. This usage does not come from the scholastic *corpus-anima distinction,* but rather is derived from the New Testament *psyche* and the Hebrew *nephesh,* which denote the deepest and most mysterious aspects of the human person being acted upon by God. I use the word "soul" in this same sense.

Note 5. Together with Teilhard (and John) I recognize the traditional Christian usage of the term "passivity" to denote our attitude of loving receptivity with regard to the divine transforming and purifying activity within us. Generally, however, I translate *passivité* by "receptivity" (a less equivocal word in English than "passivity"). Teilhard frequently uses the term in the plural (*les passivités*) to refer to a whole complex of events which befall a person: hence, that which we receive, undergo. In these instances I habitually retain the word "passivities."

Note 6. There are two pecularities of my own with regard to the terminology employed in this book: (1) I consistently use the traditional Christian terms "deification" and "divinization" in place of the more current word "sanctification." Deification and divinization denote more explicitly our movement towards transforming union in love with God. (See *Contemplation,* pp. 13–20). And (2) I consistently employ the word "stop" in an unusual way: e.g., the stop of the will on some creature. Within the basic analogy of a pilgrim's journey to God and in him, the term "stop" describes more graphically the effect of attachment to a creature than do some of its synonyms, like "fixation."

Abbreviations

AE	Teilhard de Chardin, Pierre. *Activation of Energy*. New York: Harcourt Brace Jovanovich, Inc., 1970.
Ascent	St. John of the Cross. *The Ascent of Mount Carmel*. Various editions, publications and translations.
Canticle	St. John of the Cross. *The Spiritual Canticle* (second redaction). Various editions, publications and translations.
CE	Teilhard de Chardin, Pierre. *Christianity and Evolution*. New York: Harcourt Brace Jovanovich, Inc., 1971.
Contemplation	Nemeck, Francis Kelly and Coombs, Marie Theresa. *Contemplation*. Wilmington: Michael Glazier, Inc., 1982.
Cor.	Whitman, William, trans. *Pierre Teilhard de Chardin and Maurice Blondel: Correspondence*. New York: Herder and Herder, 1967.
DM	Teilhard de Chardin, Pierre. *The Divine Milieu*. New York: Harper Torchbooks, 1960.
Flame	St. John of the Cross. *The Living Flame of Love* (second redaction). Various editions, publications and translations.
FM	Teilhard de Chardin, Pierre. *The Future of Man*. New York: Harper Torchbooks, 1964.

HE	Teilhard de Chardin, Pierre. *Human Energy.* New York: Harcourt Brace Jovanovich, Inc., 1969.
HM	Teilhard de Chardin, Pierre. *The Heart of Matter.* New York: Harcourt Brace Jovanovich, Inc., 1978.
HU	Teilhard de Chardin, Pierre. *Hymn of the Universe.* New York: Harper and Row, 1965.
Journal	Teilhard de Chardin, Pierre. *Personal Journals: I–XXI, 1915–1955.* Unpublished.
LT	Teilhard de Chardin, Pierre. *Letters from a Traveller.* New York: Harper and Row, 1962.
MM	Teilhard de Chardin, Pierre. *The Making of a Mind.* New York: Harper and Row, 1965.
Night	St. John of the Cross. *The Dark Night of the Soul.* Various editions, publications and translations.
PM	Teilhard de Chardin, Pierre. *The Phenomenon of Man.* New York: Harper Torchbooks, 1961.
SC	Teilhard de Chardin, Pierre. *Science and Christ.* New York: Harper and Row, 1968.
TF	Teilhard de Chardin, Pierre. *Towards the Future.* Harcourt Brace Jovanovich, Inc., 1975.
Writings	Teilhard de Chardin, Pierre. *Writings in Time of War.* New York: Harper and Row, 1968.

Receptivity

Introduction

This book has been a long time in the making. Not that the research which it embodies was all that difficult or drawn out, but rather that its underlying question has persisted in me as far back as I can remember. The philosophers of old refer to this as "the problem of evil." The irreligious express it: "If God is really so good and provident, how do you account for so much pain, injustice and death in the world?" Everyone at one time or another has cried at least in his/her own heart: "Why, Lord? Why must I suffer?" Even the mother of Jesus lamented on a particular occasion: "Son, why have you done this to us?" (Luke 2:48).

From an early age I tended to gravitate toward authors who, in one way or another, addressed this question in a positive and constructive manner. Yet experience proved to be the best teacher. All around me and deep within myself I could see, feel, intuit a great deal of good emanating from suffering, pain, even death. And my faith confirmed it. But how could this be? Why?

The various explanations of this truth offered by the authors I had read left me ultimately unsatisfied. This restlessness in turn forced me to search further and deeper, for my faith and my experience were seeking a better understanding of this mystery.

It was inevitable that one day I should come across the writings of St. John of the Cross (1542–1591). No one has ever succeeded in putting the dark night of the soul in more positive light than the Mystical Doctor himself. It was about this time also that I stumbled upon some essays on this general subject by

Pierre Teilhard de Chardin (1881–1955). In an instant I knew the definitive direction in which the rest of this quest would take me. In the combined insights of these two great men we have one of the most profound and far-reaching approaches to the mystery of receptivity—our innermost attitude towards God in all that we must undergo—that has ever been written. What remained, however, was for someone to bring together the insights of these two masters.

Thus was conceived the search (and the research) which, after much pain and contradiction, after many setbacks and rejections, after even several deaths and peregrinations across two continents, finally gave birth to this book. So, if at first sight this study looks like a scholarly work, please know that the context of its composition and its real purpose far transcend any purely academic endeavor. This work is truly the fruit of a persistent and deeply personal quest which came to pose itself in these terms: What could possibly be the positive and perfective value of all that we must undergo throughout life—especially of all that we must suffer and die to?

1. The Scope of this Study

Among the recent thinkers who have tried to fathom the mystery of receptivity one would certainly have to recognize the contribution of Père Teilhard. Works on this eminent French scientist and mystic are numerous and varied. Yet to date no one has attempted a comprehensive study of his insights on the many dimensions of this mystery. A number of treatises on various aspects of his spirituality do exist, yet not one tries to synthesize and evaluate the full extent of Teilhard's teaching concerning the role of receptivity in our divinization.

Most knowledgeable people would quite readily associate the name of Teilhard with activity: an active or apostolic spirituality. In effect, one still occasionally runs across the criticism that "de Chardin" (as many English-speaking persons mistakenly refer to him) is too activity-oriented, foolishly optimistic or downright naive about building up the Body of Christ. In reality, however, he never lost sight of the primacy of receptivity, not only in the spiritual life, but also in all life. For even as a young man Teilhard readily admitted how essential are *les passivités:* "In spite of the fundamental importance I have always tended to give human effort and development, I recognize that the soul does not even begin to know God until it has really had to suffer diminishment in him. So, abandon yourself to our Lord. Let yourself be swept along by him."[1]

The principal subject of this study is, therefore, an aspect of Teilhard's spirituality. But we shall also be comparing this aspect to its counterpart in the mystical theology of St. John of the Cross. The reason for this comparison is twofold. First of all, Teilhard himself suggests its importance. Yet even had he not so indicated, such a comparison would still be necessary in order to authenticate the veracity of his spiritual insights with respect to the teaching of the Mystical Doctor of the Church.

A. Reflections by Teilhard on John of the Cross

One would hardly consider the co-reformer of Carmel a spiritual mentor of Teilhard, since his references to John are comparatively few and far between. Nevertheless, they do extend over a period of thirty-two years and have a bearing on his interior development. We shall group these remarks chronologically: (1) after World War I; (2) after the composition of *The Divine Milieu* (1927); and (3) after World War II.

(1) After World War I

In an entry of his *Journal* dated December 22, 1923, Teilhard opposes what he remembers having read of John of the Cross back in 1917: "They [John and others] look upon the World as unnourishing and so conclude that God must give himself in complete substitution for it." God wipes it out, as it were. "Let us close our windows on the World and the divine light will shine within us." Teilhard then goes on to present his own position: "God gives himself to us by *assimilation* of the Real (by shining through, by sublimation, by a certain 'transubstantiation'). God illumines by way of synthesis—beyond light. . . . This latter solution is based on a profound metaphysics of Being and of Love."

Since Teilhard's knowledge of Spanish was quite limited, he could not have read John in the original Castilian. Did Teilhard then encounter John in some nineteenth-century French translation, or did he merely read about him in some unidentified, possibly even Jansenistic, commentator? We do not know. What is apparent, however, is that Teilhard appreciated some and misunderstood other key notions of the co-reformer of Carmel.

Teilhard indicates for the first time what he understands by "nights" in a paragraph written shortly after his "retreat of demobilization."[2] In this reflection he interprets well what John means by the purification of the soul: "*The nights* (deaths). In order to attain the Universal Element (Christ) hidden in the innermost being of all creatures, we must not only complete them, but we must also pass all the way through them as if through a series of successive layers. This passing through. . . . is a detachment, a night, a death." He continues: "As we arrive at each successive layer, we find that it is all resplendent with the Divine Presence abiding deep within it. But later, after we have advanced further, we discover that the Divine is no longer in that zone *for us* (it has become obscure). We must then be detached. For it is by means of successive attachments and detachments that God emerges *for us*" from within us.

Let us note two details couched in these texts (details which differentiate Teilhard from John of the Cross). First, Teilhard insists not only on detachment from and renunciation of the stop of the will on a creature, but also upon the *completion* and the *use* of the created being as necessary to the mystical life. Second, Teilhard does not ordinarily employ the expression "dark nights." He prefers rather the symbol of a Presence so diffuse or of a Synthesis so simple that it is impossible to know them adequately or to express them clearly.[3] In other words, Teilhard tends to accentuate the positive and constructive aspects of all created beings, and therefore has difficulty with John's explanation of the dark night of the soul as he understood it: namely, as being supposedly devoid of completion and use, depleted of Presence and Synthesis.

In a paper drafted for Maurice Blondel in December 1919, Teilhard criticizes in passing an ascetical attitude which he attributes to the co-reformer of Carmel: This "form of *renunciation* is that of a *cutting off,* a *rupture* with the world, an *evacuation* pure and simple of the old man. St. John of the Cross understood literally seems to conceive of the Night in just that way. Do you want to find God? Then close the avenues which let in the false exterior life. Once you have done this, *ipso facto* the higher light will appear, while the other one vanishes. The exterior noise having ceased, you hear the other voice in your heart. For there are *two* entirely distinct lights illuminating you. There are two different words reverberating continually within you. To discern the one properly you must extinguish the other. The new Earth. . . . succeeds the old Earth by pushing it aside and taking its place."[4]

Thus, prior to 1926, when St. John of the Cross was proclaimed Doctor of the universal Church in all matters ascetical and mystical, Teilhard's attitude towards his doctrine of the night can be summarized in these four points:

(1) Teilhard searched into the reality which John calls the "dark night," and (2) he perceived quite well its underlying mystery. But (3) he vigorously reacted against a form of renunciation

that he believed he saw in the literal sense of certain Sanjuanist texts, without however (4) rejecting what we may term the spirit of the mystical night. "Detachment and human effort do harmonize," Teilhard insists. "Moreover, there is no limit to their variety and combination. Vocations are limitless and in each life one finds an infinity of phases. There is within the Church St. Thomas Aquinas and St. Vincent de Paul side by side with St. John of the Cross."[5]

(2) After the Composition of The Divine Milieu (1927)

In a brief but important essay entitled *The Road of the West: Towards a New Mysticism* (1932), Teilhard observes the following: "It appears that the mystical history of the West can be described as a lengthy endeavor by Christianity to recognize and separate within itself the two fundamental ways of spiritualization: the Eastern and the Western. That is, respectively: *suppression* and *sublimation*. . . . Many have tried to find in this duality two essential and compatible constituents of holiness. But they are in reality nothing more than the vestige of two irreconcilable attitudes. Carried along and corrected by the general movement of Christianity, persons like St. John of the Cross have undoubtedly lived in actual fact a mysticism reducible to that of the sublimation of creatures and their convergence in God. But the manner in which they have expressed themselves (or at least the way others have interpreted the expression of their experience) is still decidedly 'Eastern.' "

By "Eastern" Teilhard means an approach to mysticism which accentuates suppression, withdrawal from the World, negation of creatures: in other words, the opposite of a mysticism based on love, union and transformation.[6] Teilhard concludes his thought with this observation: "We must have the honesty to recognize that in this aspect of their sanctity they are no longer meaningful to us."[7]

6

In the above passage Teilhard does acknowledge that John is a most authentic model of Christian mysticism, at least in the way in which he lived. However, certain expressions used by John in his writings to describe his personal mystical experience, together with the interpretations given by some of his commentators, leave the impression—according to Teilhard—of a doctrine irreconcilable with that of the sublimation of creatures and their convergence in God.

If such were indeed the case, then we would have to agree that at least that aspect of the Mystical Doctor is no longer appropriate for our times. However, beyond the appearances of certain passages, is not the role of creatures in our divinization—*explicit* doctrine in the writings of John—radically positive, dynamic and unitive? We shall see that it is so.

(3) After World War II

Between 1945 and 1951 Teilhard's thoughts return several times to the co-reformer of Carmel.

On August 25, 1945, in an entry in his *Journal,* he poses this question (without, however, giving himself a response): "A case of 'complementarity'. . . . the mystical passivity of a John of the Cross?"—the complement being, according to the context, his own theology of receptivity.

In a major essay entitled *My Fundamental Vision* (1948), Teilhard twice and without qualification designates St. John of the Cross as a model of the very mysticism of loving union and transformation which he himself teaches.[8] This mysticism is clearly that which he terms "the Road of the West."

On February 1, 1950, in his *Journal,* Teilhard deals schematically with the Sanjuanist term *nada* in a context which treats of the mystical act of love.

On January 15, 1951, again in his *Journal,* he poses this question (once more without giving a response): "Is a 'night' necessary prior to the mysticism of 'passing all the way through'?"

Finally, in *Some Notes on the Mystical Sense* (1951), Teilhard attempts to clarify an obscure paragraph in an earlier essay in which he had mentioned John of the Cross.[9] His clarification reads: "Both in theory and in practice Christianity not only follows, but *is* the Road of the West. Yet, we must recognize that. . . the Judeo-Christian mystical current has had some difficulty in breaking away from a perspective which has sought *Oneness* too exclusively in *Separateness* rather than in the *Unifying and Transforming Power* of God. God *over and above* all things (rather than God *in* and *through* all things). This attitude brings about a veritable 'impoverishment' of our mystical theology. . . for it is not sufficiently universal and cosmic. There are, however, some notable exceptions: Eckhart, Francis of Assisi, St. John of the Cross."[10]

Teilhard's views and questions concerning the Mystical Doctor can be reduced to these six: (1) He grasps well the essence of the mystery which John calls "night." Yet, (2) Teilhard criticizes the letter—the actual verbal expression—of the Sanjuanist doctrine of purification, which he considers static and too negative. Nevertheless, (3) he does recognize in John's lived experience a model of that mysticism which has at its core the sublimation of creatures and their convergence in God, although he does not perceive these same qualities in John's writings. However, (4) towards the end of his life, Teilhard does not hesitate to consider without qualification St. John of the Cross as equal to St. Francis of Assisi in that which pertains to an authentic Christian love of creatures. (5) As for loving union with God, he wholeheartedly recognizes the unique contribution of John to the understanding of Western mystical theology. Finally, (6) Teilhard is led one day to question himself concerning the possible complementarity of his own conviction regarding receptivity to God in comparison to the mystical passivity of St. John of the Cross.

Teilhard's attitude towards John underwent a gradual development without, however, any significant change of view.

8

Although he saw in the Sanjuanist mysticism of transforming union an exemplary formulation of the Christian mystery, Teilhard still never felt completely at ease with John's manner of expressing the theology of purification. Moreover, Teilhard clearly wished to make his own contribution to the Church's mystical tradition—a contribution not only in comparison to the co-reformer of Carmel, but also in relation to all the spiritual masters who had preceded him on the Road of the West. That is, he attempted to contribute by means of complementarity, trying to focus explicitly on certain aspects of this mystical tradition which up to his time at least had far too long remained in the background.

B. Three Questions Examined in this Study

Among Teilhard's comments on John of the Cross, two criticisms merit special consideration: (1) Teilhard viewed John's theology of the role of creatures in our interior progress as neither positive in itself nor relevant to our times. (2) John's manner of expressing the reality of the night appeared to Teilhard static and too negative. A first question we shall take up, therefore, is this: What actually is the role of creatures in our sanctification, and how does the purifying process produce unifying results according to the Mystical Doctor?

Teilhard himself considers John of the Cross a necessary point of reference for any authentic mysticism. Thus, he is aware of the importance of John's doctrine as a standard for comparison with his own. Now, if Teilhard's teaching on passive purification is truly Christian, there must then be points of convergence between the two mystics. A second question is this: What then is the core of his theology concerning receptivity, and does convergence indeed exist between John and Teilhard on this subject?

A third question may be posed this way: Has Teilhard made a personal contribution to the understanding of the mystery of Christian receptivity?

Thus, our immediate concern in this book is to study what it means to be receptive to God in the mystical theology of Teilhard. The corresponding doctrine in the writings of St. John of the Cross is set forth for two reasons: *on the one hand,* to explore the possibility of finding in his teachings of the night something other than "cutting off, rupture with the World, evacuation pure and simple of the old man." And *on the other hand,* the Mystical Doctor will serve as a necessary point of reference for authenticating Teilhard's own teaching on receptivity.

Our ultimate concern in this book, however, is this: that, having studied receptivity in John and in Teilhard and having compared their respective insights, we ourselves may come to a heightened appreciation of this mystery so essential to true growth in Christ and so integral to loving union with God.

2. The Outline of this Study

Our research unfolds in three phases: (1) John of the Cross, (2) Teilhard de Chardin, (3) divergence between and convergence of the two mystics.

The basic movement underlying these three phases is that of a dialectic. Whether the expression is "the Ascent of Mount Carmel" or "the Law of Complexity-Consciousness," in both instances a dynamic process is at work. The intricacies of the theories of evolution certainly never occurred to John of the Cross. Nonetheless, he truly lived and gave expression to the profound dynamics latent within his Christian faith. As for Teilhard, did not the core of his originality even in the scientific realm proceed also from his profound Christian commitment?

The faith life of the Church is not only in evolution, it is especially in *genesis*.[11] Indeed, it is in *Christogenesis*.[12] Over the centuries, long before Darwin or Huxley, true Christian mystics had been spontaneously swept along by a movement emanating from deep within the Gospel. This movement ascends relentlessly towards the Parousia. The dynamism of Christ has always been at the very soul of Christian mysticism, with the person of Jesus its Way, its Alpha and its Omega. The various components of a genesis can be viewed chronologically and divided into past, present and future. Or they can be discerned more profoundly in the phases of their dialectic movement so as to be distinguished in their divergence and convergence. I have chosen the latter approach, from which emerges the outline found in the table of contents.

Notes from Introduction

1. *MM*, Jan. 11, 1919, p. 275.
2. *Journal*, Mar. 31, 1919. His retreat was March 16–23 near Lyons.
3. See *Writings*, pp. 70-71, 117-149; *HU*, pp. 19-37, 41-55, 59-71; *DM*, pp. 112-149; *HM*, pp. 39–58, 61–77, 82–102.
4. *Cor.*, p. 31.
5. *Cor.*, p. 35.
6. See *TF*, pp. 40–59, 101–106, 134–147, 199–205, 209–211.
7. *TF*, pp. 51–52.
8. *TF*, pp. 194 (note 30) and 201.
9. The essay is: "Two Converse Forms of Spirit" (1950), in *AE*, p. 225.
10. *TF*, pp. 210–211. Teilhard's insistence on the immanence of God (ie., attaining him *en et à travers toutes choses*) in no way diminishes his conviction of the absolute transcendence of God (ie., the fact that he remains always infinitely distinct from, superior to and *au-delà* his creation). See *AE*, pp. 97–127, 215–227; *CE*, pp. 56–95; *HM*, 15–16, 39–58.
11. "Confusion often exists between what is called 'evolution' and what is called 'genesis.' Evolution can be directionless, periodic, in any-which-way (at least in theory). . . . But genesis is evolution directed towards a point of consummation" (Teilhard, letter to Fr. Fleming, May 19, 1954).
12. In the actual economy of salvation the point of ultimate consummation is the person of Jesus Christ. See *HM*, pp. 82–102; *CE*, pp. 76–95, 237–245; *TF*, pp. 212–215.

Phase I

St. John of the Cross

Preliminary Remarks

An initial perusal of the works of the Mystical Doctor can easily shock the uninformed reader. Take, for example, these sentiments expressed in the *Ascent of Mount Carmel.*

In order to mortify and put to rest our "natural passions" we must first "seek always to be inclined":

> Not to the easiest, but to the most difficult.
> Not to the most delightful, but to the most distasteful. . . .
> Not to the most, but to the least. . . .
> Seek not the best of temporal things, but the worst. . . .
> Desire to enter into complete detachment, emptiness and poverty
> with respect to everything in the world [for the sake of Christ]. [1]

Diligent practice of the above may suffice to enter into the night of sense. But if you honestly wish to intensify the action of grace within yourself, much more is required:

> Try to act with contempt for yourself, and desire that all others
> do the same. . . .
> Endeavor to speak disparagingly of yourself, and desire that all
> others do likewise. . . .
> Seek to have a lowly opinion of yourself, and desire that all others
> have the same. [2]

And, as if that were not enough:

> To reach enjoyment in all, strive to enjoy nothing. . . .
> To arrive at being all, will to be nothing. . . .

15

For to pass from all to all, you must be stripped of all in all.
And when you possess all, you must do so without desiring anything. . . .
Only in this nakedness does the spiritual soul find its peace and
   repose. Since it covets nothing, nothing fatigues it in straining
   forward, and nothing causes it to close in upon itself.[3]

From an initial exposure to such texts a barrage of questions
surges: Is not this way of *nada* more narrow than the Sermon on
the Mount? Are not these expressions but typical Mediterranean
exaggerations—hyperboles peculiar to the Castilian temperament?
How can one who takes them literally avoid suffering for the
sake of suffering? Must we not at least recognize that this Sanjuanist asceticism pertains to a vocation so rare, so unique, that
it is for all practical purposes extinct?

An adequate response to these questions would surely require
more than two brief chapters. So, rather than attempt a direct
answer, I shall synthesize the gist of these sayings of John to see
what bearing they have on this study.

The expression of the first two series of statements is obviously quite negative. The third series on the other hand accentuates
the dialectic between *todo* and *nada*. This dialectic situates the
negative aspect in relation to the positive thrust which dominates
the entire purifying process. That is, in the Sanjuanist perspective
deification is accomplished by means of a dialectic, the negative
aspect of which can be explained only by its radically positive
source and goal.

Before studying in more detail the process of this purification
(in chapter 2) let us first examine creation as the milieu in which
and through which this dynamic operates (chapter1).

Notes from Preliminary Remarks

1. *Ascent,* I, 13, 6.
2. *Ascent,* I, 13, 9.
3. *Ascent,* I, 13, 11-13

Chapter 1

The Positive Yet Purifying Role of Creatures in Our Divinization

An element of doctrine rarely emphasized by his commentators, but which explicitly exists in the writings of St. John of the Cross, is the positive and perfective role of creatures in our sanctification.

Indeed, there are passages and expressions of the Mystical Doctor which can be interpreted as demanding a cutting off from creation. Even if, in order to give these texts a more balanced meaning, we attempt to analyze carefully their literary and historical contexts together with their cultural and religious milieus, certain very real difficulties still remain. For example, what does John mean by *la cárcel del cuerpo?*[1] Do phrases like *actos torpes*[2] express a personal contempt for normal sexual movements, or were they simply the usual manner of speaking at his time? And the list goes on: *nada son y menos que nada, humano y bajo,* etc.[3] Both John and Teilhard were quite aware of the problems of interpretation that their writings would surely cause, and each author in his own way cautioned his readers accordingly.[4]

However, our approach in this study will not take the form of a polemical discussion of such particular questions. Rather, we intend to focus solely on basic principles.

1. Some General Observations

In order to discover the profound meaning and providential place of creation in the process of divinization in the theology of St. John of the Cross, we turn our attention to the *Spiritual Canticle*.[5] The poem begins abruptly with the anxious cry of the soul in search of its Beloved:

Where have you hidden yourself,
Oh my Beloved, having left me in anguish?
You fled like the deer,
Having wounded me.
I went forth searching frantically for you, and you were gone.[6]

This first stanza sets the tone for all that follows. When God opens our hearts more deeply to himself, we experience a painful wound of love. This wound becomes manifest in the agonizing realization that the Beloved has suddenly vanished without warning. Thus, we experience ourselves being immersed in an ever more obscure and confusing condition. We set out anxiously searching.

Previously, we had felt quite secure, very self-confident and self-reliant. Divine consolations and abundant perceptible graces were commonplace. We were basking in the pleasure of God's radiance. Then, without warning or apparent reason, this whole world of divine consolation disappears. What we had naively assumed to have been God is not he at all. We experience ourselves lost, abandoned, truly alone with *nada*.

Meditation on these verses of the opening stanza of the *Spiritual Canticle* enables us to experience through a certain empathy some of the sentiments which must have passed through John's heart in his Toledan prison. But also transparent in these verses are the lineaments of the interior journey of each and every one of us in the course of our deification.

"Where have you hidden yourself, oh my Beloved?" That

is: "Oh Word, my Spouse, show me the place where you are hidden." In this prayer we ask God "for the manifestation of his divine essence, because the place where the Son of God is hidden. . . . is the bosom of the Father. . . . which is concealed from mortal eyes and hidden from all human understanding."[7]

In this way, the *transcendence* of God constitutes the first source of the pain of absence. The deeper God draws us into loving communion with himself, the more we are forced to acknowledge that he completely transcends all we can ever know or experience of him. God so surpasses our powers of perceiving, attaining and feeling that we are left in a state of panic. God is experienced as far away. The pain of this realization is intensified because up to this threshold in our interiorization we had felt so intimately close to God. Now, at least on the level of sensory recognition, all has changed, and we fear that the change may be for the worst.

But John does not belabor the fact of God's transcendence here, since it should be evident to any spiritual person. He emphasizes instead the other essential yet rarely accentuated element of doctrine: namely, the paradoxical experience of the absence of God by reason of his *immanence.* "The Word, together with the Father and the Spirit, is hidden in essence and in presence within the intimate being of the soul. Consequently, the person desiring to find God must go forth from all created things according to affection and will, and enter within him/herself in deepest recollection. . . . God is hidden within the soul. It is there that the true comtemplative must seek him with love" and in faith.[8]

In other words, God is so overwhelmingly yet subtly present within us that we can no longer find him as before. Our search for God is now mistaken on three accounts: (1) We persist in seeking something from him, of him, rather than God in himself. We are still preoccupied with feeling good about our prayer, with being consoled in our spiritual life, with knowing precisely on which rung of the ladder of interior progress we are situated.

(2) We continue looking for him everywhere except where he is truly to be found. We are still looking for him in sensory manifestations, in fond memories, in creatures both within and outside ourselves. The true God must henceforth be found in dark faith deep within the intimate being of our person, there abiding in transforming and purifying love. And (3) we insist on searching for God in a manner that can never approach the real him. We are still searching for him by our own efforts, with our own initiative, out of our own system of "should's" and "should not's." In a word, we are still trying to get something out of God, rather than humbly receiving God himself.

What does the Mystical Doctor mean by the expression "all created things" *(todas las cosas)?* Time and again John uses this or an equivalent phrase to refer to absolutely every created being, whether natural or supernatural, whether in heaven or on earth, whether personal or nonpersonal. In other words, the phrase "all created things" denotes every being that is not God himself, whether the creature is capable of being divinized, is an instrument of divinization or is already divinized. We must eventually go forth from them all, even from this earthly existence. There are no exceptions!

"To go forth from all things according to affection and will" is also a constant refrain in the vocabulary of John. Note that he insists that we must *go forth* from all things. He does not speak of *withdrawing* from anything. The accent falls on the positive movement towards God, in God, rather than away from some thing. Furthermore, there is not the slightest indication—either in John's life or in his writings—suggesting that the contemplative person (and there is truly a contemplative dimension in each of us) should or even can dispense with the normal and providential need of creatures in the process of interiorization. Nonetheless, because of the relationship of creature to Creator and because of the internal laws of movement from scatteredness to transforming union, the way of true spiritualization demands an unqualified detachment of the will with respect to all that is not God himself.

John furnishes an apt example of the need and providential use of created things on the one hand, together with complete renunciation of the will with regard to these same creatures on the other. Citing several authorities from Scripture concerning the mortification of the appetite, he quotes the Vulgate rendition of Luke 14:33: *Qui non renuntiat omnibus quae possidet, non potest meus esse discipulus.* Then he goes on to translate this logion of Jesus for his reader. As he does so, he carefully adds to it his own personal interpretation: "Whosoever does not renounce *with his will* everything he possesses cannot be my disciple."[9]

That is to say: What we must renounce above all is not the creature as such, but rather our will in regard to the creature. Even though in a general sense all creatures do exist to assist us in our quest for God, the actual presence or absence of any particular creature does not of itself directly help or impede that search. Whether it aids or not depends entirely on our inner attitude (our "will") towards the creature. Thus, the will attaching itself to a creature that is present or coveting something or someone that is absent—in other words, stopping itself on any creature whatsoever—can never go all the way to the goal of its search for the one true God.

In another context John had explained why this is so: "What we call 'night' here is the mortification of the will with respect to all created beings. . . . We are not speaking of the privation of created things themselves, since this would not in fact strip the soul if it coveted them. Instead, we are treating of the detachment of the will and appetite for them. It is precisely this which leaves us free and disencumbered of anything created, even though we may actually have that creature in our possession. Nothing created can occupy the soul nor directly cause it harm because none can enter into it. Rather, it is the will and appetite for creatures which can do it much harm."[10]

The object of detachment, therefore, is not the creature itself, but rather the *stop of the will* upon the creature—a stop which

21

obstructs our passage all the way through creation to God in himself. For God is God. He is not his creation. Yet he abides within the innermost being of every creature while continuing to transcend it entirely. Consequently, the person who would encounter him truly must pass all the way through creation.

As for the image "to go forth," John explains it this way: "This spiritual departure may be understood first as a going forth from all things through contempt and aversion for them; secondly, as a going out of oneself through forgetfulness of self."[11]

These sayings of the Mystical Doctor have a very negative ring indeed. Taken literally, one must ask how Christian such an attitude really is. Furthermore, the very image of a going forth in this context raises a question: If one must find God within oneself, would it not seem more normal to *enter into* oneself rather than to go out of oneself? This problem does not escape the attention of John either, for earlier he had stated that in order to perfect the union of love already established between the soul and God "it is fitting for the soul. . . to enter within itself in deepest recollection," communing there with God in love.[12]

What then is meant by this analogy of a spiritual departure from all things and from oneself in order to enter more deeply within oneself for the sake of communing there with God? It means this: God is infinitely beyond yet intimately within each creature. The creature is *of* God and *to* God. Given the proper nuances, it is also capable of being divinized. Nonetheless, the creature is not God himself, nor does it contain him, strictly speaking. The privileged place where each of us ultimately finds him is the intimate center of our being. There God dwells in us in love.[13]

This discovery is realized in a positive manner through contemplation and in a negative manner through the complete purification of the person with regard to everything created (him/herself included). The concentration of this *purifying contemplation* is upon the human will in such a way that God communicating himself to us consumes in love every trace of egocentrism and removes every attachment (stop), whatever it may be. Thus, God abiding within our deepest selves breaks the impasse of selfishness, regardless of its form or manifestation. If we have gone out of our egocentrism, this is not in order to shun any of our gifts, but rather with these same gifts to pass on to God through all.

From a practical point of view, one of the most difficult elements of this going forth is that of getting past the defense mechanisms which we have consciously or unconsciously built up over the years. These defenses constitute formidable obstacles to progress in God. And perhaps it is for this reason that John attacks them with such vehemence: "through contempt and aversion for creatures; through forgetfulness of self."

Having made these general observations, we now move on to develop more specifically the positive contribution of creatures in the process of purification.

2. The Positive Role of Creatures in Greater Detail

Several times St. John of the Cross uses the following literary device: He begins with an abrupt and sometimes startling statement which captures the attention of his readers. He then follows this up with a more ample explanation in order to establish the context in which his initial assertions can be more properly understood. The purifying role of creation in our sanctification, as presented in the *Spiritual Canticle,* is an application of just such a methodology.

John begins the *Canticle* very abruptly: "Where have you hidden yourself, oh my Beloved?" In the opening stanza he describes in just twenty-two words of powerful poetry one of the most complex and perplexing experiences on our journey towards union: the apparent absence of God by reason of his overwhelming presence within us. This experience, so concisely expressed by

John, caps a long personal history of divine preparation within each of us and can be correctly appreciated only when situated within a broader mystical and theological context. Having captured the reader's attention, John then proceeds to fill in that context in stanzas 2–7 of the *Spiritual Canticle*.

Throughout these six stanzas (2–7) he specifically treats of the knowledge *(conocimiento)* of creatures. He addresses in successive order self-knowledge, knowledge of nonpersonal creation and knowledge of persons. The meaning that he gives the term "knowledge" is derived from the biblical usage of the word: namely, experience. Thus, John is stressing our providential need for deep and direct personal involvement with the creatures in our life. In the case of knowledge of persons, he is referring to deep and direct interpersonal involvement.

John's first step in constructing the broader theological context of stanza 1 consists in what might be called the beginning of adult spiritual life (stanzas 2–3): the phase of self-knowledge, active purification and discursive prayer.

Undoubtedly, the single most important creature in the life of each of us is our own self, our very personhood. It is there that all transformation and purgation must begin. Our person is the core where God abides in love. It is the matrix of all his salvific activity in our regard.

The basic principle underlying John of the Cross's theology of self-knowledge and mortification is this: The more we come to experience our true self together with God in us, the more we perceive the obvious stops of our will on certain creatures. What positive action can we take in order to get moving again? We mortify our will and appetites with respect to the creature in question. John goes on to spell out the nature of this mortification: Christian renunciation is basically a positive reaction on our part with respect to our own self-knowledge. This reaction should affect our involvement in/with the created in such a way that we become more mature (ie., less attached). This detachment must attain not only the will, but every facet of the human person. All desires, pleasures and enjoyments undergo intense purification. Every attachment must become detached.

Even though this mortification arises from a positive need and awareness within us, we nonetheless experience it quite painfully. The most obvious source of this pain is the realization that nothing created can ever again bring back the Beloved as before, since God is calling us forward into ever deeper mystery. In this condition, the searching soul directly addresses creation with this anxious cry:

O forests and thickets,
Planted by the hand of my Beloved,
O meadows of green
Adorned with flowers,
Tell me, has he passed through *[por]* you?[14]

Some translators render the *por* of the Spanish text "by" rather than "through." This is an unfortunate and misleading choice of terms. John is stressing that the Word passed *through* creation in virtue of his incarnation, death and resurrection. He did not just pass it by or pass it up. Therefore, the true follower of Christ must do likewise. In our journey to God, we too must pass all the way through creation, not circumvent it.

The above stanza marks a new threshold (a more intense interiorization) in our quest. Now "the soul begins to journey through the consideration and knowledge of creatures to knowledge of its Beloved, their Creator. Indeed, after the exercise of self-knowledge, this experience of creatures is the next step along this spiritual road to knowledge of God."[15]

In response, creation recognizes the gifts it has received from its Creator as well as their place in his plan:

Pouring out a thousand graces,
He passed through *[por]* these groves in haste.

And beholding them as he went,
With his glance alone
Left them all clothed in beauty.[16]

Yes, he passed through creation in haste: that is, without stopping, without getting hung up, without becoming attached to anything or anyone anywhere along the way.

In the next stanza (6), John elaborates in some detail upon his understanding of the role of creation in our divinization. He introduces his remarks in this manner: "In the living contemplation and knowledge of creatures, the soul beholds the immense fullness of graces, virtue and beauty with which God has gifted them."[17]

This observation is not of course particular to St. John of the Cross, since any person of good will should perceive as much. However, building upon this basis, John offers a deeper insight. At a certain threshold in the process of spiritualization, God dwelling and operating from deep within our innermost being intensifies his transforming activity to the point of thrusting us more profoundly into the obscure way of the night. The role of creatures, without shifting direction, then becomes more acutely and decisively purifying. Thus, "the soul—wounded in love by this trace of the beauty of its Beloved, a beauty that it has experienced in creatures, and anxious to see this invisible Beauty—speaks the following verses:

'Who has the power to heal me?
Cease surrendering yourself to me in this manner.
Do not send me
Any other messenger,
Since they cannot bring me what I yearn for.' "[18]

The truths underlying this stanza may be summarized in this manner: Because God is immanent in his creatures, the more we experience creation in its depths, the more we know *of* its Creator. An increase in the knowledge of God through his creatures causes an intensification of love for him. This in turn increases the yearning for the presence of our Beloved in himself and for complete union with him.

But there is even more to this mystery. This deeper experience of God through creation not only brings about an increase in love, but it furthermore effects an increase in suffering. In becoming more conscious of God, we see all the more unmistakably that no creature, however excellent it may be, is the One whom we relentlessly seek. Only the Beloved can fulfill in perfect and consummated love the inexhaustible yearnings of the human heart. In this way we are wounded ever more painfully by our thirst to be possessed completely by God on the one hand, and on the other by the inability of any creature to give him in the plenitude we crave. This wound of love hollows out a painful vacuum within us which only God in himself can fill.

The more we are drawn into transforming union, the more deeply we experience the wound of love. St. John of the Cross speaks of three successive phases of this wounding in relation to ever intensifying spiritualization: *herida* (a surface wound: *Canticle,* 1) *llaga* (a deeper wound: *Canticle,* 7) and *cauterio* (wound by fire: *Flame,* 2).

In other contexts, John treats amply of the wounds we inflict on ourselves by self-love and self-indulgence—the wounds of false love, as it were. But in our present context he is speaking of the wound caused by mature love of God through his creatures. This wound comprises in essence the impossibility of the human person to become completely satisfied by anyone or anything other than God in himself. Thus, the term "wound of love" does not refer to some form of dissatisfaction nor to the result of negative or regressive attitudes or experiences. It refers to the normal and providential consequence of authentic Christian involvement.

Fully conscious of this wound of love, the soul laments: "Who has the power to heal me? Which means: Among all the gratifications of the world, all the satisfactions of the senses, all the pleasures and delights of the spirit, certainly nothing can heal me, nothing is able to satisfy me. . . . Not only do all other things fail to satisfy the soul. . . but rather they increase its hunger and appetite to see him as he is in himself. Thus, the glimpses of the Beloved which are obtained from knowledge, from feeling or from any other communication whatsoever are like messengers which teach something about him, quickening and exciting the appetite more, as do crumbs in an intense hunger."[19] But they cannot ever bring God in himself to us.

The Sanjuanist theology of the cross inherent in this perception of creation is profoundly positive. True Christian appreciation of creatures causes an emptiness, an absence which only God himself can fill. In this manner, the creature as creature accomplishes its role perfectly. It demonstrates experientially that it is entirely from God and to God without ever becoming God. Furthermore, real knowledge of and mature affection for creation are not only tolerable; they are providentially necessary so that we can experience within ourselves even more acutely the positive void which this very knowledge and love produce.

Once God has brought us through the threshold of spiritual adulthood, he takes possession of us even more directly, but always in a manner which enhances our individual freedom. He accomplishes this progressively with our active participation. Thus, to the degree that we seek him, God himself quickens and directs this same search by the loving wound of his absence, which wound derives from his transcendent immanence.

From a certain point of view this absence of God is a sort of optical illusion. In reality he is more present and more directly operative within us than ever before. Yet, from another point of view, this sense of distance is very real. For God is wholly Other. Each deepening encounter with him in faith through creatures intensifies this realization. Thus, deeper awareness of the immanence of God serves only to increase our appreciation of his utter transcendence. The immanence of God always remains transcendent.

Having enabled us to taste the splendors of creation, God then causes us to experience unmistakably through this encounter our inexhaustible yearning to abandon ourselves unreservedly to him, our Creator. In this sense the images of abyss, of hunger, of thirst serve to accentuate the consciousness of our limitless receptivity to God. Only the person who is stopped on some creature is, so to speak, engulfed or imprisoned. The soul who proceeds on its way towards God through creation reaches its goal. Its heart is becoming ever more opened to the One-Thing-Necessary (Luke 10:42). Thus, creatures fulfill their mission: the finite has opened the human heart to the Infinite. The created has made us more consciously receptive to the Uncreated.

The Mystical Doctor summarizes this chapter of the *Canticle* with a moving prayer: "Lord, my Spouse, what you gave of yourself to me in part, give now entirely. And what you show in glimpses, show now in full light. . . . communicating yourself by yourself. It appears at times in your visits that you are going to give me the jewel of possessing you. Then, when I examine myself more carefully, I find myself deprived of you in the manner I crave to have you. . . . Therefore, surrender yourself now giving yourself completely to all my being, so that I may possess you totally. Henceforth, cease sending me messengers who do not know how to tell me what I seek. . . . Nothing in heaven or on earth can give me the experience I so pine to have of you. . . . Instead of these messengers then, Oh Lord, may you yourself be both the Messenger and the Message."[20]

The seventh stanza of the *Spiritual Canticle* both concludes John's presentation on the positive role of creatures in our sanctification and at the same time introduces a deeper phase in the wound of love. In stanzas 4–6, he had been referring principally to nonpersonal creation: what we would call "things." However, in stanza 7, John treats specifically of involvement with persons other than oneself.

Endowed with intelligence, free will and immortality, personhood is the crown of creation. Our mature love for another person, therefore, carries with it much deeper potential for experience of God. This, in turn, causes such an increase in the wound of love that John even changes the word for wound (*herida* in stanzas 1–6) to *llaga* (in stanza 7).

Thus, in the theology of the Mystical Doctor, not only is nonpersonal creation necessary in the process of our gradual transformation in God, but persons together with personal involvements and commitments constitute an even more crucial service in opening us to uncreated grace. Creation, especially personal creation, is essential to the actualization of our receptivity to God in himself.

Obviously the complete teaching of St. John of the Cross concerning creation is not included in this brief presentation. Nonetheless, what we have presented serves to highlight the dynamics and the positive dimension that he emphasizes with respect to the role of creatures in our divinization. This positive accent underlies his many negative expressions and puts them in proper perspective. Thus, the criticism made by Teilhard concerning this element of John's spirituality—criticism expressed in *The Road of the West* (1932)—is not justified.

In order to summarize what has been expressed above and to introduce what follows, we cite a passage from the *Night* (II, 9, 1). These lines explain particularly well the purpose of the dark night of the soul in its relation to everything created: "Even though this blessed night[21] darkens the spirit, it does so only to impart light in all things. And even though it humbles us and reveals our miseries, it does so only to exalt us. And even though it impoverishes us and empties us of all our possessions and natural affections, it does so only that we may reach forward divinely to the enjoyment of everything in heaven and on earth, all the while preserving a general freedom of spirit in them all."

Notes from Chapter 1

1. "The prison of the body" (*Ascent*, II, 8, 4).
2. "Dirty [lascivious, disgraceful, impure] acts" (*Night*, I, 4, 1–8).
3. "They are even less then nothing" (*Ascent*, I, 4,3); "Human and consequently lowly" (*Night*, II, 16, 4).
4. See *Ascent, Prologue*, 1, 8–9; and *Writings*, p. 272; *letter to Valensin*, July 15, 1929.
5. Most of the stanzas of the *Cántico* were composed during his imprisonment in Toledo, Spain (1578). John's commentary on the poem was written in 1584 after the *Ascent (cir.* 1579–81) only to be followed by a second and definitive redaction *cir.* 1587–1588.
6. *Canticle*, stanza 1.
7. *Canticle*, 1, 3.
8. *Canticle*, 1, *6.*
9. *Ascent*, I, 5, 2.
10. *Ascent*, I, 3, 1–4.
11. *Canticle*, 1, 20.
12. *Canticle*, 1, 6.
13. The analogy of "center" for John is consistent with Western mysticism: namely, a loving movement towards the Center who is Christ. This is a transforming and unifying concentration: *engolfarse en el centro (Night*, II, 20, 6). Thus, "center" is not a spatial or mathematical term, but rather one which denotes the utter open-endedness of pure quality as in the expression: *en el centro de su humilidad* (Ascent, I, 13, 13).
14. *Canticle*, stanza 4.
15. *Canticle*, 4, 1.
16. *Canticle*, stanza 5.
17. *Canticle*, 6, 1.
18. *Canticle*, stanza 6, *1* .
19. *Canticle*, 6, 3–4.
20. *Canticle*, 6, 6–7.
21. *Esta dichosa noche*: the *beata nox* of the Easter Vigil proclamation.

Chapter 2

Purification as Essential to Union with God

This chapter examines certain specific aspects of the dark night of the soul according to the Mystical Doctor. Together with the previous chapter, this one will serve as a basis for comparison with Teilhard's theology of receptivity. The presentation also responds indirectly to Teilhard's remarks: a misguided "form of renunciation is that of a cutting off, a rupture with the World, an evacuation pure and simple of the old man. St. John of the Cross read literally seems to conceive of the night in just that way."[1]

When one speaks of John of the Cross and purification, one spontaneously thinks of the dark night. This phrase refers to his eight-stanza poem, *En una noche oscura,* written within several weeks of his prison break. It evokes also the two commentaries he began on that poem, but never completed: *The Ascent of Mt. Carmel* (cir. 1582) and *The Dark Night of the Soul* (cir. 1585). The phrase, furthermore, denotes the doctrine which occupies such a central place in all his works.

The first stanza of the poem *En una noche oscura* reads:

In a dark night,
Burning in love with anguish,
—Oh happy chance!—
I went forth without being seen;
My house being already at rest.

In order to appreciate the fact that John is describing here not only a personal mystical threshold, but also a very specific historical event in his own life—namely, his nocturnal escape from prison—it suffices to stroll along *El Paseo del Carmen* in Toledo, Spain. There one can stand on the approximate spot where John, emaciated from dysentery and nine months of solitary confinement, jumped to freedom on that moonless August night in 1578. One need only see the jagged cliff which rises up from the raging Tajo River at the foot of the ancient wall of Carmel to imagine some of the indescribable terror and relief that must have filled his heart at that moment. But John does not linger on his prison break as such. Using that historical event as a kind of springboard and symbol, he concentrates instead on describing the fundamental breakthrough which results as God takes definitive possession of each of us.

Thus, the Mystical Doctor presents in moving imagery the first of four essential characteristics of purification: (1) It is down-to-earth. (2) It is received in/by the person. (3) It propels us forward. (4) It establishes us in peace.

First, therefore, purgation is always radically *concrete*, down-to-earth, permeating the person even to the most banal details of his/her daily existence. The specific form that purification takes is tailored by God to all the particulars, no matter how seemingly trivial or insignificant, of each individual's life. No one escapes the consuming fire of divine love. We all pass through the dark night, for we all must ultimately die.

A second essential dimension to purification is that we *undergo* the night. Every truly salvific action within us is received. We do not save ourselves or one another. We are saved by God.

John emphasizes this point while commenting on the fourth line of the stanza in question: "the soul goes forth—God wrenching it out—solely because of his love."[2] Our interior situation is described in this sentence by an active verb "to go out": "the soul goes forth." Immediately, however, John adds with insistence: "God wrenching it out." That is, this departure is in reality more

33

passive than active because it is God who makes us go forth. He breaks our shackles so that we can move freely out of self and more deeply into him.

The phrase "oh happy chance" is another indication of this truth. This going forth, this radical tearing out, *happens* to us. And we are indeed fortunate that it does happen! There certainly do exist what are termed "active purifications." These are the voluntary mortifications which we undertake as a result of self-knowledge. But, at best, these attain only the surface of our personhood in our struggle to overcome selfishness. God himself must directly purify us in our depths. It is the Father alone who prunes (John 15:4). Moreover, this deeper purification happens not as a punishment, but in love: "solely because of his love."[3]

A third characteristic of this night is its underlying *movement*, its inner tension toward something better. The rhythm of the Spanish text reveals an energetic procession. The verb *salir* (to go forth) indicates not only the act of leaving, but above all that of making a leap forward, that of being propelled. We are freed from certain attachments and immaturities in order to advance more directly on the way of Spirit. This is true progress.

A fourth characteristic of this night is its sense of *peace*. Peace exists in the midst and in spite of the intensity of the purification. John stresses this truth in the second and fifth lines of the stanza in question.

In the second line he juxtaposes love and anguish: "burning in love with anguish." Fear, confusion, pain—in a word, anxiety—are very intense during some phases of the night. Yet, all the while this is going on, our innermost being burns with love. Even in the most intense throes of the night of spirit nothing can ever quench the conviction that God is really in control and that he will faithfully bring all this turmoil to a peaceful resolution.

In the fifth line of this stanza John states the characteristic of peace even more directly: "My house [inner self] being already at rest [in peace]." Moreover, this occurs in (during, on, in the course of) the dark night itself.

There will undoubtedly be a profound peace after we have completed our journey through the night. But here the Mystical Doctor is stressing that in the midst of the perplexities of this purification a very deep peace already exists. This has nothing at all to do with the peace which the world might try to give. God's peace does not consist in the satisfaction of the appetites or in relaxation from tension. Rather, it is that of the purifying and transforming presence of God within us. Love, faith and hope are intensified in proportion to the intensity of the night. This is so, not because suffering of itself is capable of causing an increase of the divine presence within us, but rather because total darkness is the necessary condition for complete abandonment to God. Instead of plunging us into sheer nothingness, the night is a "happy chance"—a veritable grace—and as such becomes the most conducive milieu to facilitate the divinizing and pacifying activity of God within us. Not only can the world not bestow this peace, the world finds it impossible even to comprehend.

Thus, by reason of its essential relationship to transforming union, the night is revealed as a fundamentally positive reality. John explains it this way: "This dark night is an influence of God within the soul which purges it. . . . This we call infused contemplation. By it God secretly teaches us and instructs us in the perfection of love, without our doing anything or even understanding how this is taking place. This contemplation, as the loving wisdom of God, causes two principal effects within us: by purifying us and illuminating us, it disposes us for union in love with God."[4]

These considerations raise two important questions which bear directly on our purpose: (1) What are the far-reaching implications of the phrase: "This dark night is an influence of God within the soul"? And (2) what is the process whereby this purification is accomplished?

1. "This Dark Night Is an Influence of God within the Soul"[5]

Who/what are the causes of the night? Scholastic theology, in which St. John of the Cross was thoroughly schooled at Salamanca, distinguishes four causes: *efficient* (the agent who does something); *final* (the reason why something is done); *material* (that which is acted upon); and *formal* (that which makes something be what it is). Without posing the question in a strictly scholastic fashion, the Mystical Doctor does nevertheless treat the four causes of purification.

John's writings leave no doubt that God himself is the agent (efficient cause) of the night and that transforming union with him in love is its goal (final cause). It is also clear that the human person in all his/her concrete condition—weaknesses as well as potentialities—is, so to speak, the matter which is transformed. But, according to Sanjuanist theology, what can be ascribed as the formal or specifying cause of purgation?

The answer is not really very difficult. If the dark night is an essential element of the process of divinization, and if divinization means allowing oneself to be transformed in God by God, then his influence within us is the formal cause of our purification, just as all his activity within us is also the formal cause of the whole divinizing process. It is God himself who completely permeates the human person. We cooperate maximally by receiving God and letting him be.

Let us examine this "influence of God within the soul" more closely.

First of all, to influence means to act upon. So, if one must use a preposition to express this grammatically, one should nor-

36

mally use "upon" (*sobre* in Spanish). One exerts influence upon another. Notwithstanding, John chooses the preposition *en* to accentuate the interiority of the source of this purgation. This is a purifying influence of God from deep within the human person.

How does John envisage this activity of God? In explaining the signs for discerning the authenticity of the night of sense, he specifically addresses this question. While proposing the first sign in which we find neither satisfaction nor consolation in the things of God or in anything else created, the Mystical Doctor ascribes our aridity to this truth: God himself puts us in the dark night in order to dry up and purify our sensory appetite. Therefore, God does not allow us to find attraction or delight in any thing whatsoever. The causality described here is primarily efficient. However, John gives another sign which subtly effects the transition to a sort of formal causality: When we can no longer meditate or discourse despite our persistent effort to do so, this fact may indicate that God is already "beginning to communicate himself to us by pure spirit."[6] From the context it is clear that God communicating himself to us purifies us. This communication is purgative contemplation.

John sheds further light on this mystery by interweaving two analogies: (1) to consume and (2) to assimilate.

(1) *To consume:* "God accomplished the purgation of the soul by means of this dark contemplation. In it we suffer not only from emptiness and suspension of our natural supports and acquisitions. . . but also this dark contemplation purifies us, annihilating and emptying, or consuming as does fire. . . all the affections and imperfect habits which we have contracted throughout a lifetime."[7]

In this text, John chooses three terms to express the purifying activity of contemplation: to annihilate *and* to empty, *or* (better) to consume like fire. His arrangement of the contrasting conjunctions "and. . . or" implies that he recognizes that to annihilate can mean to destroy completely and that to empty may be taken in an entirely negative sense. So, lest he be misunderstood, John attempts to give a positive interpretation to his thought by introducing the analogy of consuming. This analogy evokes the suffering which arises out of transformation. Whatever is being consumed, as in the case of fire, is being transformed. For this reason, among the three expressions cited, John himself indicates a certain preference for the verb "to consume" precisely because of its positive connotation: "This purifying and loving divine light operates within us as does fire upon wood which transforms the wood into itself."[8]

(2) *To assimilate:* In our passage to eternal life, everything is revealed to us "because of our total assimilation to God. . . . Yet, however highly the soul is exalted before reaching this light something always remains hidden from it. This persists in proportion to what we lack for complete assimilation to divine Wisdom. . . . Love is like a fire which ever ascends upwards with a tendency towards being absorbed in the center of its sphere."[9]

All these notions—transforming union, assimilation in God, fire which ascends and consumes—converge on what the scholastics call formal causality. Yet, that in which God is causing us to be transformed infinitely transcends any classical ideas of causality. For "that in which" is really "him in whom": God himself.

At this point, an important question arises concerning the interdependence of contemplation and purification. Is it more correct to say that contemplation itself purifies, or to say that purification gives way in the end to contemplation? In other words, do we first have to be purified so that afterwards God can communicate himself to us in contemplation, or is it rather the communication itself of God to us which effects the purgation? Which really comes first: contemplation or purgation?

Obviously there is reciprocal influence. But here as always the true Sanjuanist insight is clearly more positive than negative. John explains himself with a comparison which is dear to him: that of light which paradoxically darkens. "The purer and simpler this divine light is in itself the more it darkens, empties and annihilates the soul in all its acquisitions and particular affections. . . . Yet, to say that supernatural and divine light darkens inasmuch as we receive more light and purity seems incredible. . . . Yet, this is understandable if we consider that the clearer and more manifest supernatural things are in themselves, the more obscure they appear to our understanding."[10]

How then does contemplation purify? "This divine ray of contemplation, assailing the soul with its divine light, surpasses our natural light. It darkens us and deprives us of every natural affection and acquisition which we had previously obtained by means of natural light. It leaves us not only dark, but also empty in our faculties and desires, both spiritual and natural. Leaving us thus empty and in darkness, this contemplation purifies and illumines us with divine spiritual light. All this transpires while we think that we have no light and believe ourselves to be in darkness."[11]

In this manner, God, welling up from deep within the human person, really is the cause (formal, efficient and final) of the night. Yet, the actual source of the pain which emanates from the purgation is the human condition as such in all its weakness, immaturity and selfishness. Contemplation (ie., God's direct, loving activity within us) itself purges what cannot be transformed in him. In all transformation there exist both continuity and discontinuity. Something endures beyond, while something else is broken off and left behind. God directly effects all dimensions of this mystery: the forging ahead, the breaking loose and the letting go. Nothing befalls us—not even sin—that God does not somehow make serve our metamorphosis in love (Rom. 8:28–39).

John furnishes three examples of how concretely this mystery translates into the human condition. (1) "The spirit of fornication is given to some to buffet their senses with strong and abominable temptations. . . . (2) Sometimes in this night the spirit of blasphemy is added. It commingles intolerable blasphemies with all their ideas. . . . (3) At other times the spirit of dizziness is

39

given to them, not for their downfall, but to exercise them. This spirit darkens their senses in such a way that it fills them with a thousand scruples and perplexities."[12]

Moreover, it really is "God who sends these storms and trials in this night and purification of senses." He does this "so that having been chastened and buffeted in this way, their senses and faculties may be exercised, disposed and prepared for divine union."[13]

It is not enough, therefore, to assert that the night itself is an essentially positive reality. We must also recognize that the storms integral to the night play an equally constructive role in our divinization. How can this be? How can something so potentially harmful also be so good?

Under different aspects, we experience one and the same event, both as a good and as an evil. These storms are evil inasmuch as they are painful onslaughts of sin truly living within us. Yet, they are also an incomparable good to the degree that they exercise us. Thus, when bombarded by these storms we must simultaneously resist the evil and foster the good in them. This is not only not to succumb to temptation (Matt. 6:13; Luke 11:4), but it is especially to cooperate with God in love (Rom. 8:28). In this manner, the transforming power of God is encountered through the storms and beyond the pain they cause. We can accomplish this, however, only by naked abandonment to God in faith.

Note also that God does not tempt us in the strict sense (James 1:13–14). He exercises us. These temptations and sufferings flow from ourselves. They arise from our inner being inasmuch as we have come with all our poverty and sinfulness into direct contact with the divine, transforming activity within us. Thus, the darkness of the night does not, strictly speaking, proceed from God, but from the human condition: that is, from our inability to receive God as he is in himself. We remain innately powerless in the presence of the all-loving-transcendent-immanent One. We experience our basic weakness in proportion to the force of God within us. God's transforming love systematically annihilates every trace of self-centeredness.

Therefore, the phrase "God sends these storms" indicates that the divine action within us is basically positive because it is divinizing. This phrase, furthermore, accentuates the fact that the disproportion between creature and Creator is so immense that his divine light darkens the soul; that the loving influence of God is so foreign to our egocentrism that it agitates us no end; that the power of the divine presence is so intense that it leaves us with the impression that our Beloved is absent.

How do these general principles affect individual persons in concrete life situations? The compassionate love of the Father sees to all these particulars in a way best suited to the transformation of each one. In other words, the divine will determines the duration, the intensity and the form of this "fast and penance" for each of us "in accordance with the degree of union of love to which God intends to raise us," and in accordance with the greater or lesser amount of egocentrism to be eradicated.[14]

2. The Dark Night as a Perfective Process

Under this heading we shall succinctly group four other aspects of the night according to St. John of the Cross which bear on our study: (A) the place of detachment in our purification; (B) the purpose of renunciation; (C) the role of faith in this process; and (D) the manner in which John envisages receptivity.

A. Detachment of the Will and Desire

At the beginning of the *Ascent* (I, 3, 1–4), John states the problem very precisely: "What we call 'night' in this context is the privation of *gusto* in the appetite regarding all things. . . . We are not treating here of the mere absence of things, since that of itself would not strip the soul as long as it still coveted them. Instead, we are speaking of the detachment of the will and desire *(desnudez del gusto y apetito)* for them. Only in this way are we left free and empty, even if we have them in our possession."

Outside influences do not directly attain our innermost being. Consequently, they cannot directly cause us harm. It is rather our *attitude* with regard to a particular creature which fosters or hinders our interior progress. It is not our immersion in the world which prevents us from progressing spiritually, but only the stop of our will and desire upon the created that impedes this progress.

What then does John really mean by: (1) detachment, and (2), in particular, by detachment from *gozo* and *gusto?*

(1) The Meaning of Detachment (Desnudez)

John uses a variety of words to express the attachment which must be eradicated: *gozos, gustos, apetitos, afecciones de la voluntad, asimientos,* etc. In the context of *desnudez* (detachment, renunciation, mortification, stripping, spiritual nudity) he employs these terms in a nontechnical, yet precise, manner. There is obviously no question here of denying our power to will; or of negating our natural appetite; or of destroying our ability to consent, to enjoy or to be happy. The point is rather the renunciation of all attachment with regard to all that is not God, even if the creature in question is from God and to him.

Once again we find the insightful moderation of the Mystical Doctor. This moderation is evident in the desire to make use of everything that comes from God in order to return to him without, however, stopping anywhere along the way. Yet it remains just as difficult for John as for anyone else to express with all the required nuances the complexities of the detachment process.

The texts which contain these nuances—the "and's," the

42

"but's," the "however's"—are numerous. For our purpose we shall examine only two key expressions. In each of these texts John qualifies his idea of renunciation by a carefully chosen word: (1) "the *spiritual* detachment in all things both sensory and spiritual." (2) Concerning Christ, whose example we must follow, "he died *spiritually* to what was of sense in his life, whereas he died naturally to it in his death."[15]

According to the contexts, the terms "sensory. . . . of sense" carry no pejorative connotation whatsoever. John is simply making reference to the sensory part of the soul.[16] The accent is placed on "spiritual(ly)." This nuance implies much more than nonmaterial. In effect, John emphasizes the intangible, the inexpressible, the mysterious; ultimately the "I-don't-know-what" of the *Spiritual Canticle* (stanza 7).

In short, it is a question on the one hand of a most subtle balance between love of creatures and quest for God in and through them, and on the other hand of complete renunciation of the will with respect to them all. This balance is literally a personal mystery in the life and vocation of each and every one of us.

This sense of mystery guides us from day to day, enabling us to discern whether a particular affection is in reality a loving search for God in and through his creation, or a stop on some false god. In actual fact there is always a certain mingling of these two elements every step along the way. Hence, there must be just as much detachment regarding a particular creature as there is will to love it, if we are to maintain our ascent. Moreover, true discernment as to exactly what requires detaching and in what measure remains extremely delicate. Therefore, lest we cut off something vital, we very quickly find ourselves obliged to let ourselves be purified passively by God (John 15:1–2). For we can never completely sort out the intricacies of all our wills and desires, of all our pleasures and enjoyments, of all our affections and gratifications.

This is why, in the ultimate analysis, detachment can only

mean letting oneself be carried forward by God, in God, as he unstops all stops and strips all attachments.

But the question still remains: Why is it particularly necessary to renounce *gozo* and *gusto*?

(2) The Necessity of Renouncing Gozo and Gusto in All Things

John's study of *gozo-gozar* is long and complex. For example, in the *Ascent*, the subject is treated in book III from chapters 17 to 45. What does *gozo* mean, and what principles govern it?

El gozo usually denotes spiritual joy or enjoyment. But it can also mean sensory pleasure, satisfaction or gratification. It can even designate all the above without distinction. "The first of the passions of the soul and of the affections of the will is *el gozo*, which is none other than a certain contentment of the will together with esteem for something that it considers desirable."[17]

John's fundamental principle is this: "The will must not *gozar (se)* save in what is for the honor and glory of God. Now, the greatest honor that we can give him is to serve him according to evangelical perfection. Outside this nothing is of value or profit to anyone."[18] We are called to *gozar* or not a particular creature according to the concrete circumstances of our personal vocation.

The problem of *gusto* is similar to that of *gozo*, but only more complex. *Gusto* can mean everything that *gozo* does. But *gusto*, like the English word "gusto," usually accentuates sensory excitement and exhilaration. Translators of St. John of the Cross often render *gusto* "will" in the sense that we have been using the term throughout these two chapters.

Gusto-gustar is found on almost every page of John's writings. He uses it both in a positive sense[19] and in a negative sense.[20] And there are instances where he plays on both.[21] *El gusto* in its perjorative usage is more directly related to our purpose, since it is in this context that John insists upon its complete renunciation. In this pejorative usage, he employs *gusto* not only in the sense of attached will, but also very frequently as denoting sensory pleasure and gratification. We shall examine four assertions of the Mystical Doctor:

(1) *El gusto,* like *el sabor* and *el deleite,* by its very nature tends to entrap us, turn us inward and concentrate us on self.[22]

(2) Those who by their *gusto* are still attached to their prayers, their oratories or their religious customs (such as the habit, solemnities, devotions) have not yet abandoned themselves entirely to God and are resisting the divine influence within them.[23]

(3) We "must not be attached to anything: neither to the exercise of meditation, nor to any *sabor* whether sensory or spiritual. . . for it is necessary that the spirit remain free and annihilated with regard to all things. If we desire to fix ourselves upon any manner of thought, discourse or *gusto* whatsoever, that attachment impedes us, disquiets us and makes noise, thereby breaking the deep silence that should rightfully exist within us."[24]

(4) God "strips our faculties, our affections and our senses, both spiritual and sensory. . . leaving us in deepest affliction. Thus, we are deprived of the feeling and *gusto* which we had previously experienced in spiritual blessings. This privation is one of the principles required in order to reach union of love. . . . The Lord works all this in us through a pure and dark contemplation."[25]

What is there in the nature of pleasure, delight or enjoyment that blinds us? The second and third references furnish a response: namely, attachment to any creature whatsoever. In other words, a particular satisfaction derived from a certain creature captivates us. The fourth reference gives the reason attachment causes such a problem: If we are fixated on anything—even something sacred—we are stopped in our journey to God in himself. This attitude toward a particular creature impedes the creature from fulfilling its providential role in our life. By attaching ourselves to a creature, we turn that being into a god. What then must we do to resume our forward movement? We must become detached. Or more precisely, we must let ourselves be detached by God.

John frequently uses the verb *desnudar* when speaking of detachment. In Spanish this verb can be used to express both the reflexive sense (to detach oneself) and the passive voice (to be detached). The exact meaning intended by the author has to be determined from the context. Translating *desnudar* as used by John in the context of detachment by the reflexive form only can give the false impression that we are expected to *detach ourselves* from all our attachments. Certainly we must make whatever positive contribution that is indicated by divine inspiration and common sense. But at best such actions attain only the surface of the real problem. All truly salvific purging is effected by God. We receive this interior cleansing of ourselves. It happens to us. Thus, although we may indeed *attach ourselves* to a creature, we do not in effect detach ourselves. For *desnudar* means to let oneself be detached by God: in his way, at his time. Moreover, his pruning will be infinitely more effective than anything we could ever accomplish or even imagine.

As for the question of pleasure in particular—and by pleasure we mean the sensory exultation for which joy is the spiritual counterpart—the Sanjuanist explanation for the necessity of its renunciation is this: In accordance with our ontological and psychological structure, what is sensory in the human person is necessary for the development of spirit. However, beyond a certain point, which is variable according to individuals and circumstances, whatever is of sense in a given situation tends to obstruct further interiorization.

The Mystical Doctor insists, nevertheless, that the obstacle does not proceed from *gozo* or *gusto* as creatures (any more than it flows from any other creature). There is nothing intrinsically wrong with either enjoyment or pleasure. Rather the obstacle emanates from *gozo* and *gusto* inasmuch as we are stopped on them and refuse to pass on through them to God in and beyond them.

46

Therefore, it is necessary to be stripped of and to renounce *gozo* (to the degree that it constitutes a stop) and *gusto* (in the sense of attachment) in everything created. To reach the Goal, we must mortify our *gozo* and our *gusto* regarding each creature without ever rejecting or despising the created as such. Yet, John does point out that pleasure is particularly entrapping since we all spontaneously tend to hold on to it for as long as possible. This is simply human nature. For this reason, the sincerely searching person must be especially honest, circumspect and objective—that is, mortified—where *gozo* and *gusto* are concerned.

In short, in order to reach the Goal, we must pass on through creatures. In order to pass through them, we cannot be stopped on any of them. This renunciation is concretized "actively" by mortification and is ultimately brought to completion in the "passive" night. Thus, we arrive at the peace and interior spiritual joy which the world could never give (John 14:27; 15:11).

To renounce pleasure in its most evangelical sense means this: Enjoy both that which gives pleasure and the pleasure itself. But enjoy them as from God and to him—provided of course they really are—without, however, stopping on either in any way. Examples of such pleasure may include good health (Mark 1:30–31; Luke 7:21); the intimacy of friendship (Luke 10:38–42; John 13:23); a fine wine (John 2:10). A very practical test of this honest enjoyment is our ability to delight in pleasure and to accept its loss with the same equanimity, as did Job (1:21): "Yahweh has given. Yahweh has taken away. Praised be the name of Yahweh!"

Renunciation comes about by undergoing in faith and love the diminishments which occur quite normally in the course of living (e.g., restrictions of diet, bereavements, the aging process). At God's prompting, detachment may also be accomplished by voluntarily sacrificing something, or by cutting down—even abstaining altogether from—certain goods which cause pleasure. Ultimately however, *desnudez* is effected by allowing ourselves to be penetrated "passively" by the purifying action of God in contemplation. This last form of mortification is unmistakably the most efficacious. Yet, each of the others remains necessary throughout life.

To strip, to renounce, to deny, to mortify, to detach our will and desire mean, therefore, to be led by a will and desire for God which is so intense that we simply cannot stop until we rest entirely in him. This truth is a necessary result of increasing receptivity to God in himself.

B. The Purpose of Renunciation

What is the raison d'être of purification according to St. John of the Cross? Is it primarily expiation, or is it rather the exigencies of transforming love?

John responds this way: "Even though this blessed night darkens the spirit, it does so only to impart light in all things. And even though it humbles us and reveals our miseries, it does so only to exalt us. And even though it impoverishes us and empties us of all our possessions and natural affections, it does so only that we may reach forward divinely to *gozar* and *gustar* everything in heaven and on earth, all the while preserving a general freedom of spirit in them all."[26]

The person whom God is calling to himself is a sinner. Sin and its consequences enter deeply into the mystery of our need for purification. However, the basic purpose of the night goes much deeper than expiation as such. Even though other reasons may also be ascribed,[27] the raison d'être of our purification is our existential situation vis-à-vis the uncompromising demands of our passage to transforming union.

In other words, God's loving design for us is really the primary source of our purgation as well as of the intensity of our night. If God had not called us to such an incomparable destiny— to be transformed in himself, to enjoy supreme happiness and freedom in him—there surely would be no need for such purifi-

48

cation. Transformation always means dying at least partially in what one loves. But if this dying in another must be all the more perfect the more we give ourselves to one greater than ourselves, then there can be no limits to the uprooting required on our journey in God.[28] We do not just pass from one phase of development to another (as from adolescence to adulthood). Rather we are completely and radically transformed not only to a new life, but to God's very own life and love.

This same doctrine appears even where John accentuates the specifically expiatory aspect of purgation. For instance, after citing Job 19:21 ("have pity on me. . . because the hand of the Lord has touched me"), John comments: "How amazing and pitiful it is that the weakness and impurity of the soul are such that it experiences the gentle and light hand of God so heavy and contrary to it. He only touches it, and does so mercifully without pressing it down or weighing upon it. God does this in order to pour out his graces upon us, not to punish us."[29]

C. Faith and the Dark Night

The role of faith in the process of transforming union remains without doubt one of St. John of the Cross's greatest contributions to the spiritual theology of the Church. With regard to this vast and complex subject, we shall limit our remarks to only one aspect: faith in relation to the process of purification.

At the beginning of the *Ascent* (I, 2, 1), John presents an overview of the process of spiritualization which he compares to a journey: "This passage of the soul to divine union is called night for three reasons. First, because of its point of departure" which is the innate poverty of the soul itself. "Second, because of faith which is the means or road which we must travel to reach this union. Third, because of the point of arrival, namely God" himself.

Faith is that which links together all the diverse elements of

49

the night. Faith is that by which, in which, through which the pilgrim advances, reaches the Goal and is transformed.

In a passage of the *Night* (I, 11, 4) where he alludes to Matt. 7:14, John explains: "The narrow gate is this night of sense in which the soul is stripped so that it may enter therein being united to God in faith. . . . Afterwards, the soul continues on the straight way of the night of spirit. . . so as to journey to God in pure faith, which is the means whereby it is united to him."

Faith is furthermore the principle of union with God. Faith and love unite us to God. Nonetheless, faith in the Sanjuanist perspective is dark and purifying even as it transforms. Moreover, the darker it is, the more completely it unifies. We shall never really appreciate the inner dynamics of the night until we grasp the purifying role of faith in this process. Faith as a purifying and unifying principle is a myriad of paradoxes.

Faith is the fundamental cause of the night, while remaining our only guide through the same night. Stanzas 3, 4 and 5 of the poem, *In a Dark Night,* illustrate especially well this mystery:

> In this blessed night,
> In secret, when no one saw me
> And I could see nothing,
> Without other light or guide
> Than that which burned in my heart.
> —Stanza 3

There comes a point in the night when literally everything goes dark. Not even reason can serve as a guide any more. All that we have at this time is the flame of faith, hope, and love which burns unremittingly in the innermost recesses of our being. These virtues are truly "like a fire burning in my heart, imprisoned in my bones" (Jer. 20:9).

> This guided me
> More surely than the light of noonday
> To a place where he awaited me

—He whom I knew so well—
A place where no one appeared.
—Stanza 4

This intensely obscure faith guides us through the perplexities
and anxieties of the night with a deeper peace than the certitudes
of reason could ever furnish. Yet, assuming that our Beloved is
just around the next corner, we discover on arriving there that
he is still further up ahead. Moreover, each experience of being
drawn closer to Christ is always different from the previous one.
Each encounter is more mysterious, more faith-laden, more
obscure to our mental faculties and senses. This is so true that
he whom we thought we knew so well is simply no longer there.
The true God is always beyond. . . .

O night that guides me!
O night more lovely than the dawn!
O night that united
Beloved with lover,
Lover transformed in Beloved!
—Stanza 5

The overpowering darkness of faith becomes itself the source of
incomparable peace and strength. Faith is both the guide to and
the ultimate principle of transforming union.

Faith is also both light and night. It darkens by virtue of its
overwhelming brilliance (like being blinded by looking directly
at the sun).[30] As divine light, faith simultaneously illumines and
purifies us. In fact, it purifies us by illuminating us, since it
illumines by way of kenosis (Phil. 2:7). That is, it reveals who
God is not, and it enlightens us regarding our own inner poverty
together with the innate limitation of every other created being.
Faith as divine light is not of itself obscure, even though its
overwhelming force necessarily produces an obscuring effect
within us mortals. Thus, nothing created can adequately convey

it: The eye has not seen, the ear has not heard—it has not even so much as entered our imagination who God is in himself (1 Cor. 2:9).

As the night of faith intensifies, it progressively eradicates every attachment. In this way, by a process of elimination the true face of God is made manifest. In letting go all that he is not, we experience him more deeply face to face and thereby live more fully (Gen. 32:31). Nevertheless, this mystical communion between God and the soul in faith causes an even more intense darkness, for he is unmistakably experienced as nothing *(nada)* that can be grasped, held on to, comprehended in any human fashion. God is truly the Ineffable, the Inexpressible, the "I-don't-know-what" of the *Spiritual Canticle* (stanza 7).

This darkness of faith is the necessary and providential condition in the progression of our total abandonment to God. Ultimately, this condition wrenches every trace of egocentrism from us. Obviously, the darkness as such does not cause the abandonment of faith. God alone is the cause of faith and of its intensification. Yet, the obscurity resulting from our poverty vis-à-vis the divine force within us is the condition *sine qua non* in which true surrender takes place.

In other words, to the degree that a given creature is not affected by obscure faith, we try spontaneously to cling on to it. It is as if that particular creature were a ray of sensory light in an otherwise dark and mysterious tunnel. This phenomenon is so for reasons profoundly entrenched within the human psyche. The human person spontaneously resists obscurity and seeks out what s/he considers certitude, clarity and order. This darkness, however, elicits a most positive response on our part. For the less we can see, cling to, attach ourselves to, the more we necessarily plunge into the mystery of the divine Person up ahead. To cling is to reach behind, to hold on to something or someone for dear life. Faith is sheer leap forward; pure risk in God. Thus, faith increases in proportion to the intensity of the darkness of the night, up to and including death itself. Death is our final leap into total darkness. And yet in death we end up in total Light.

In this manner, faith conceals God, while uniting us with him.[31] Faith is the very lifeblood of purgative contemplation.[32]

Faith is God's gift. It is that which he bestows on us, enabling us to respond to his initiative. The most salvific response that we can give is commitment: the return-gift of ourselves to God.

The logia of Jesus and the writings of St. Paul are replete with declarations that faith is the commitment of that which is deepest and most ineffable in our person to that which is deepest and most mysterious in the personhood of God (Father, Son and Spirit). The Gospel consistently requires that the true disciple not only believe *what* Jesus proclaims, but especially that s/he believe *in* Christ Jesus himself: "Do you believe in the Son of Man?" (John 9:35). The difference is that of believing someone or of believing *in* someone. It is the difference between merely accepting the veracity of another and fully committing oneself to the other's person. In this sense, faith and love constitute the basis of all interpersonal relationships, transformation and union. In this sense too, faith is necessarily obscure since it is commitment to that which is truly most *mysterious* in the Other. In this sense, finally, faith is loving response, rather than intellectual assent.

In short, faith is gift; faith is commitment. Faith is both light and night. Faith guides and conceals, illumines and darkens. Faith strips us while uniting us to God. He wells up from within gently drawing us forward. God gives himself, communicating himself without ever being exhausted. Faith empties us in such a way that nothing precise or particular remains to which we can cling. What is left is *Todo*, who completely possesses us without himself ever being totally possessed. God does not come to fill a void. He was always there. Everything that is not God has become, in/by faith, *nada*.

D. The Meaning of Receptivity in St. John of the Cross

Teilhard consistently uses the noun *passivité(s)* to denote our attitude of receptivity toward God's transforming activity within us. Although the corresponding noun *pasividad* does exist in Spanish, the Mystical Doctor does not ordinarily use it. He does, however, employ the adjective *pasivo(a)* and the adverb *pasivamente* in the traditional Christian mystical sense of loving receptivity. Yet, whatever the actual expression, the leitmotif of all John's teaching remains this: Everything that is done within us in order to divinize us is done by God. We, in turn, receive all this in love, letting it be done while actively contributing to the process whatever God indicates should be done.

To illustrate this truth we shall examine four passages. Each contains its own particular nuance.

(1) The first passage is situated in the context of contemplation: "Often the soul finds itself in this loving and peaceful presence. It does not work actively at all with its faculties. . . . It simply receives" God. "Nonetheless, it will sometimes need to make quiet and moderate use of discourse in order to be better disposed" for contemplation.[33]

This last sentence reveals a subtle dialectic between activity and receptivity within the person. Before purifying contemplation definitively takes over, considerable effort is usually necessary in the realm of discursive prayer. This activity proceeds from God's initiative within us, and also precedes his more intense operation within us. In a subsequent phase, when we are more passive, we must sometimes return to a limited activity in order to become more receptive.

John continues: "But when the soul is led into contemplation, it must no longer work with its faculties, because at this time. . . understanding and delight are produced in the soul, not by its activity, but by its loving attentiveness to God and by its remaining without any desire to feel or to see anything."

54

This last sentence stresses the attitude of deep, mystical receptivity which we maintain in contemplation. This has absolutely nothing to do with laziness, idleness or inertia. Moreover, once we are drawn into receptivity of a superior order, we must make every effort not to make any effort at all. All we have to do is to wait, remaining as open as possible to the divine activity within us. This is required because "God is now communicating himself passively to the soul just as light is communicated to a person who has his/her eyes open."

In this communication of God to us, our effort to remain attentive is the spiritual, receptive effort of making no physical or mental effort at all. It is simply letting go, really abandoning ourselves to God. What God does within us is so penetrating and so transcendent that the best we can do is to do nothing, surrendering ourselves lovingly to him who dwells within.

(2) The second passage is in reference to *padecer* which means to suffer, to endure, to undergo in love. John uses this word very frequently to stress the transcendent excellence of the way of utter receptivity: "Another reason why we walk securely through the night is this: we advance *padeciendo*. The way of *padecer* is more secure and more profitable than that of enjoyment and activity. First, because in *el padecer* God supplies the strength, while in our enjoying and our activities we exercise our weaknesses and imperfections. Secondly, in *el padecer* we are exercised and acquire virtues. We are purified, made wiser and more prudent."[34]

(3) The third text accentuates the intense and consistent receptivity necessary in a contemplative vocation: "When the soul desires to remain in interior peace and leisure *(ocio),* every act, affection or desire wherein it may then seek to indulge will distract it, disquiet it and make it feel aridity and emptiness of sense. The more we attempt to find support in affection or knowledge, the more we experience the void which can no longer be filled in that way." John then adds: "Contemplation is nothing other

than a secret, peaceful and loving infusion of God" himself within us, "which, if we allow it, enflames us in the spirit of love."[35]

(4) Finally, the dynamics of love pertain par excellence to the mystery of receptivity: "The spirit experiences itself intensely and passionately in love. . . for since this love is infused, it is more passive than active. Thus, it generates in the soul a strong passion of love. This love, because it already possesses something of union with God, participates to some extent in those properties which make it more the actions of God than of us. These properties are received in us passively. Here we simply give our consent."[36]

For St. John of the Cross, the notion of passivity (receptivity) is used in opposition to activity. This is true when John is speaking of passivity both in the sense of remaining receptive to the divine activity within us and in the sense of remaining passive in relation to any created action which we ourselves could perform. But passivity especially derives its meaning from passion/passionate. In the context of contemplation, the word "passive" (receptive) means being enflamed with love, becoming fully alive in Christ: "I live now, no longer I, but Christ lives in me" (Gal. 2:20). To receive passively, not to work actively, to love passionately all mean, therefore, to allow God to open us in order to permeate us completely. It is God himself who does all. We let it be done (Luke 1:38). By doing nothing we are in actual fact doing our very best. For by abandoning ourselves wholly to God, we cooperate fully.

Thus, everything that is done within us in order to divinize us is done by God. We in turn receive all this in love, letting it be done while actively contributing to the process whatever God indicates should be done.

3. Summary

Throughout these two chapters we have examined two essential aspects of Sanjuanist mysticism: (1) the positive role of creatures in the process of sanctification, and (2) the positive thrust of the night, which consists in its necessary relationship to the process of transforming union. Two basic conclusions flow from these considerations.

First, this truth: God is revealed and communicated to us only in an actual kenosis of ourselves and of everything created. This is true in virtue of our personal incorporation into the integral mystery of Christ: his incarnation, death and resurrection. In light of this mystery, the positive role of creation is to open our hearts to the Uncreated. The finite is meant to point us beyond itself to the Infinite. This opening is effected by way of *nada*, which consists in essence in this mystical experience: God is nothing created.

Second, kenosis is truly a process, a development. We do not, strictly speaking, enter into it. Rather we are permeated and swept along by it. The most efficacious way for us to cooperate with this movement is, therefore, to let ourselves go in order to let ourselves be united to God, by him.

Notes from Chapter 2

1. *Cor.*, p. 31.
2. *Ascent*, I, 1, 4. "—*Sacándola Dios*—": *sacar* means to extricate, to force out with determination, to tear out.
3. *Solo por amor de él (Ascent*, I, 1, 4). John intends both senses of *de él*: God's love for us and our love for him.
4. *Night*, II, 5, 1.
5. Some translations unfortunately render *una influencia de Dios en el alma* by "an inflow(ing) of God into the soul." John is stressing the activity of God from *within* the person, a welling up (John 4:14); not an "inflow" from the outside.
6. *Night*, I, 9, 4–8. See *Contemplation*, pp. 60–71.
7. *Night*, II, 6, 5.
8. *Night*, II, 10, 1.
9. *Night*, II, 20, 6. In a context where he is accentuating the mystical dimension of the Omega Point, Teilhard twice evokes the model of John of the Cross and uses the following terms to describe what he and John have in common in contrast to Oriental mysticism: "Pantheism of union (and hence of love). Spirit of 'tension.' Unification by concentration and hyper-centration to the center of the Sphere," "My Fundamental Vision," 1948, in *TF*, p. 201).
10. *Night*, II, 8, 2. Ibid., II, 10, 1–10.

57

11. *Night*, II, 8, 4. Ibid., II, 16, 10–12.
12. *Night*, I, 14, 1–3. See *Contemplation*, pp. 85–89.
13. *Night*, I, 14, 4. See *Contemplation*, pp. 89–96.
14. *Night*, I, 14, 5.
15. *Ascent*, II, 1, 1 and II, 7, 10. The stress is mine.
16. John consistently speaks of *la parte sensitiva del alma* (*Ascent*, I, 1, 2) rather than the sensory part of the body: *la noche y purgación del sentido en el alma* (*Night*, I, 14, 1).
17. *Ascent*, III, 17, 1.
18. *Ascent*, III, 17, 2. By "evangelical perfection" John means living the Gospel deeply, whether in religious profession or not. The verb *gozar* can be translated by: to enjoy, to take pleasure in, to derive satisfaction from, etc.
19. E.g., as in the interchange between the Beloved and his spouse: *gustándolo El, lo da a gustar a ella, y gustándolo ella lo vuelve a dar a gustar a El, y así es el gusto común de entrambos* (*Canticle*, 37, 8).
20. E.g., *Flame*, 3, 73.
21. E.g., "In order to be able to *gustarlo* all, you must desire to have *gusto* in nothing" (*Ascent*, I, 13, 11).
22. See *Ascent*, III, 10, 2–3. *Sabor* means: savor, taste, pleasure. *Deleite* means: delight, joy, satisfaction.
23. See *Ascent*, III, 24 and 38; *Night*, I, 6.
24. *Flame*, 3, 34.
25. *Night*, II, 3, 3.
26. *Night*, II, 9, 1. Ibid., II, 16, 7.
27. E.g., so that the appetites themselves may attain their proper perfection and accomplishment (*Ascent*, I, 4—10); "according to the degree of union in love willed by God's mercy" (*Night*, II, 7, 3; ibid., I, 14, 5).
28. See *DM*, p. 88.
29. *Night*, II, 5, 7.
30. See *Ascent*, II, 3, 1–6.
31. *Ascent*, II, 4, 1–8; *Night*, I, 11, 4.
32. See *Ascent*, II, 10, 4.
33. *Ascent*, II, 15, 2–5. (The same for the subsequent quotations.) See *Contemplation*, pp. 27–52, 72–75.
34. *Night*, II, 16, 9. See *Contemplation*, p. 113.
35. *Night*, I, 10, 5–6. See *Contemplation*, pp. 97–109.
36. *Night*, II, 11, 2.

Phase II

Père Teilhard de Chardin

Preliminary Remarks

In responding indirectly to certain criticisms of Teilhard regarding the writings of St. John of the Cross, we have indicated in the previous two chapters that the work of the Mystical Doctor does explicitly contain a most positive teaching concerning the role of creatures in our divinization. Moreover, he explains how the purification essential to this process is fundamentally dynamic and unitive. These two elements of his spirituality are perennially valid. Hence, they are also of the utmost importance to every Christian in our time.

In these same chapters we have also set forth certain points that can serve as a basis of comparison between the doctrine of receptivity in Teilhard's spirituality and the basic elements of the Sanjuanist night. This comparison will not be made in the form of a synopsis of more or less parallel passages or vocabulary. Instead, our comparison will highlight the fundamental points of convergence and divergence between Teilhard and John of the Cross. Since their respective theologies are formulated independently, we set forth their teaching on the subject independently of each other. We have already discussed John's position. We now move on to Teilhard's. The comparison itself will be presented in the conclusion of this study.

Teilhard approached the question of *les passivités* in a manner consonant with Christian mystical tradition: namely, to designate our receptive attitude towards God as we undergo his transforming and purifying activity within us. In *The Divine Milieu* (p. 75),

Teilhard expresses his understanding of receptivity in its broadest terms: "That which is not done by us is by definition received in us." He connects the noun "passivity" with the verb "to pass into," as in: "The power of Christ has passed into me"; and with the adverb "passionately," as in: being more passionately in love with Christ Jesus.[1] This understanding of receptivity is in continuity with a theme which goes back to his earliest writings: "Christ had overwhelmed both me and my Cosmos."[2] Thus, Teilhard's theology of receptivity is profoundly linked with his Christology, especially with the mystery of the passion of Jesus: "When we suffer: (1) We suffer Christ, and (2) Christ suffers in us. We suffer together *[com-patimur]*."[3]

The term *passivité(s)* is found most frequently in his essays and correspondence between the time of his tour of duty during World War I and the composition of *The Divine Milieu* (1927). It occurs principally in contexts which treat one or other aspect of the mystery of interior detachment or which involve some other painful experience. Often Teilhard employs the expression *les passivités* without any qualifying word. In certain contexts, however, he does specify a particular form of receptivity. I shall arrange my treatment of this mystery according to the three basic forms which Teilhard designates and which I develop in chapters 3, 4 and 5.

Notes from Preliminary Remarks

1. See for example *DM*, pp. 111 and 127.
2. "The Priest" (1918), in *Writings*, p. 216.
3. *Journal*, Feb. 28, 1919.

Chapter 3

Passivities of Existence

Teilhard uses the expression *les passivités de l'existence* for the first time in a letter to his cousin Marguerite.[1] In this letter he discerns two essential components of our contribution to "the Real:" (1) That "effort without which a certain portion of being would never be realized," and (2) those "powerful energies which force even our staunchest resistances to bend before them and acknowledge their mastery." The efficacy of these energies arises from the fact that they make us undergo "the creative and formative action of God who alone has the power to detach us from ourselves." These passivities "establish in us something that is not of us." They are *"in nobis, sine nobis."* Teilhard epitomizes his sentiments this way: "Oh, the joy of experiencing the action of the Other within us! That is precisely what makes the passivities of existence so delicate and so worthy of adoration, since through them God asserts his primacy over us."

In other words, there are two essential and complementary components of our contribution to reality (i.e., to the actual world into which God has purposely brought us): personal effort and the passivities of existence. These passivities are energies—a whole complex of influences—which overwhelm us, forcing us, contrary to some of our innate tendencies, to yield to Someone who completely surpasses us. These passivities constitute an es-

63

sential element of the creative and re-creative action of God, since they form the only force powerful enough to detach us from our egocentrism. They impart to us something of the Real, which otherwise we could not attain.

The phrase "passivities of existence" refers to the transforming and purifying action of God deep within the human person. This phrase accentuates the purgative aspect of that activity, for in undergoing God more intensely we necessarily also suffer more acutely than ever our inner poverty. The word *passivité* denotes our fundamental disposition of receptivity and availability with respect to the divine presence within us and all around us. Because God asserts his primacy over us through these passivities, they are worthy of adoration. Furthermore, they produce profound joy even though we undergo intense suffering proportionate to our resistance, imperfection and selfishness.

Teilhard's views, expressed above, accord remarkably well with those of St. John of the Cross which were treated in the previous chapters. But there is this notable difference: Teilhard formulates his teaching within a vocation which is decidedly active. He is conscious of a call to build up the Earth. John, on the other hand, expresses his doctrine within a way of life that is decidedly contemplative. His was a call into ever increasing solitude. This difference of concrete milieu and of personal charism explains perhaps one of the nuances that Teilhard gives to the prepositional qualification "of existence" in the expression "passivities of existence." This qualifying phrase is equivalent to another phrase which he frequently employs: "of the Real."

Teilhard explains what he means by "Real" in the essay *The Mystical Milieu* (1917): "In the initial phase of the mystic's movement in God, the experience of him present in all things presupposed an intense *zest for the Real*. A little later, immersion in God operative in all things forced him/her to develop as broad a consciousness as possible, *again of the Real*. And now that s/he is progressing further into the immanent God, s/he is committed as a person to an unremitting fulfillment, *always of the Real.* This can mean only one thing: we are inexorably forced by our passion for union with God to give all things their *highest possible degree of Reality*, of existence, whether it be in our knowledge and love for them, or in our proper being. Thus, from the depths of his/her rapture in God, the true mystic is ever *a supreme Realist!"* [2]

During the months it took to write *The Mystical Milieu,* Teilhard reflected many times on his own interior life and on his particular gifts. In his *Journal* (March–August 1917), he expresses the belief that God had given him mystical graces. Teilhard entertained no illusions at all about the role of such mystical phenomena as visions, levitations and locutions in the process of spiritualization. Nor did he give the slightest indication of ever having experienced any of these during his life. But he was convinced that he had received the sober mystical gift of being an indefatigable searcher for the Real; for the One-Thing-Necessary; for the Universal; for the Consistent; for the Absolute: for God in himself. "My lifeblood is to live and help others live the mysticism of God in all." A couple of years later, again in his *Journal* (February 19, 1919), he becomes even more explicit: "My inner strength, my sole force is to be 'mystic.' "

The determinative "of existence" (in the phrase *passivités de l'existence*) evokes still another meaning: The human person actually exists in order to become more. We are in tension becoming. In view of the Christ-event, this becoming is not just towards a vague, nondescript "more." It denotes transforming union in God himself. For this to be effected, we must fully undergo Christ. The very fact that we exist then carries with it the call to be in a way which completely transcends whatever we could become of ourselves. Thus, we receive not only our initial act of existence, but also the entire complexity of re-creative energics which comprise transforming union.

The expression "passivities of existence," therefore, refers

65

to all the creative and formative graces which constitute the core of the purifying action of God within us. They are called "passivities" because of our receptive attitude towards them. They are in us, in spite of us. These passivities are qualified by the phrase "of existence," since without them we could neither attain the fullness of our own being-becoming, nor efficaciously foster the highest possible degree of the Real in them.

Every true mysticism is above all a lived experience, a living mystery. In the case of Teilhard, this truth is especially obvious. The unfolding of his interior life not only comes through in his writings, but also his spiritual journey remains their best interpreter. For these reasons, and also to illuminate the origins of the receptive element in his spirituality, we shall examine certain turning points in the early and mid-life of Teilhard, wherein he experienced the passivities of existence in a particularly intense manner. These turning points are grouped under two headings: (1) certain thresholds in the genesis of his interior vision, and (2) his spiritual crisis during the battle of Verdun.

1. Certain Thresholds in the Genesis of Teilhard's Interior Vision

At the age of thirty-six, in *My Universe* (1918), Teilhard made a concise first attempt to trace the genesis of his "interior vision." This vision comprises "the earliest and most essential characteristics of my 'view of the World' together with the successive stages of my complex interior attitude." Reflecting on this, he observes: "As far back as I can remember (even before the age of ten), I can distinguish clearly within myself the presence of a dominant passion: the passion for the Absolute. . . . This expressed itself in an insatiable need to rest unceasingly in Something tangible and definitive. And I sought everywhere for this blissful object. In fact, the history of my interior life can be said to revolve around the development of this search directed as it was upon realities ever more universal and perfect."[3]

Then, at the age of sixty-nine, Teilhard tried again to synthesize the major components of his interior vision. This time, in *The Heart of Matter* (1950), he identifies the axis of continuity of his life as "the Sense of Fullness" or "Pleromic Sense," thus coining a term derived from a New Testament expression used in reference to Christ (John 1:16; Eph. 1:23; Col. 2:9). These phrases delineate his quest and irresistible need for "the unique, all-sufficing and necessary Reality" (Luke 10:42). This need is born of the conviction that within him, but without him, something essential exists to which everything else is only accessory. This grace can rightly be called mystical, and it impressed itself upon his consciousness in unmistakable fashion: "Once it has been experienced, it is impossible to confuse it even in the least degree with any other passion of the soul. . . . For it is of a superior order." Thus, what Teilhard calls successively "Sense of Consistency, Cosmic Sense, Human Sense, Christic Sense," is merely the account of a gradual explication which evolved within him of this essential element expressed in ever richer and more refined ways.[4]

What exactly were some of these ever richer and more refined ways?

They revolve around what he termed in later life "the call of Matter," or more precisely, "the call of Something burning at the heart of Matter."[5] Reminiscing back to the age of six or seven, Teilhard notices that he was already a searcher. Whereas most children of that age would be lost in a world of make-believe, he found himself seeking out a solitary corner of the family property in order to "contemplate the savored existence" of his "God of Iron." Curious behavior for such a little boy, wouldn't you say? And why iron, of all things? Teilhard himself smiles as he recalls these events. But he was dead serious at the time. It was not just any piece of iron either. It had to be massive and heavy—like a plow or a statue or a column—in order to attract

67

his "adoration." Thus, in his childish perspective, through the symbol of iron he sought that which must be lasting and durable: in a word, immortal. Nonetheless, to the child's despair, he realized one day that iron rusts and corrodes. It was not he whom his heart sought with such ardor.

The setback, however, was only momentary. For it had the effect of a catalyst, forcing him to search further and elsewhere for something more consistent. This time rocks attracted his attention. But not just any rocks. They too had to be massive, huge, indestructible, like the immense boulders in the mountains of his native central France. But alas! Even these boulders occasionally broke loose and came crashing down into the valleys below, shattering into a thousand pieces. So he had to search ever further. This time Teilhard was thrust in the direction of the planetary, which in turn progressively brought him "towards the vision of the Universal and the discovery of Evolution," and finally to the "inner awakening to Cosmic Life" (i.e., to a divine call emanating from the Heart of Matter; to a divine Person transforming Matter from within).

Thus, from iron to rocks to the cosmic, Teilhard's quest produced in the end "the awakening and development of a dominant and victorious Sense of All." *Todo*.[6]

In this brief summary of certain thresholds in the genesis of Teilhard's interior vision, several features of the passivities of existence are striking. First, there is his irresistible and progressive quest for more and more. This need always to search further is within him, without being of him. Yet it remains intimately linked to his own voluntary cooperation with this inner Force.

Second, each threshold crossed towards the more and more is effected within a painful detachment of self. This detachment proceeds from two interrelated sources: (1) from the progressive intensity of the action of God within him (i.e., God exerting his primacy over him), and (2) from the purification emanating from that transforming presence. In this manner, Teilhard is placed directly on the road towards true fullness of being-becoming.

This last point deserves a more detailed examination. Two examples from Teilhard's early adult life serve to illustrate how adversity brought him directly into contact with deeper values: (A) the death of his older brother Alberic; and (B) a dead end: the cult of inert passivities.

A. The Death of Alberic

In *My Universe* (1918), and in *The Heart of Matter* (1950), we discover several passages which reveal Teilhard's personal horror in the face of corruptibility: "As a child, the flesh of Our Lord appeared to me as something too fragile and too corruptible." "Pathetic despairs of a child! To find one fine day that iron corrodes, that steel rusts. . . . As a consequence of their apparent frailty, living beings greatly disquieted and disconcerted my childhood. . . . The physical-chemical instability of organic substances, and more particularly of the human body, shocked my need for consistency in spite of intellectual evidence to the contrary."[7]

In the eyes of young Pierre, everything which corrupted seemed to cease existing. Corruption (mortality) was equivalent to disappearance of being. This attitude is easily understandable from the perspective of a youth enthralled with nature. However, the setbacks caused by the decomposition of his cherished matter incited Teilhard to go through and beyond the appearances. He continued to search for the Incorruptible not exactly in matter, but rather at the *Heart* of Matter.

It is difficult to reconstruct exactly the interior upheavals of a young boy, but the thread which at that time ran through all this restlessness is undoubtedly the mystery of death. Teilhard had seen death at close range several times during his formative years, but one death in particular wrenched him to the very core of his being: the passing of his eldest brother Alberic on September 27, 1902.

Teilhard's reflections on this death reach us from Cairo in 1905. In a dozen or so letters to his parents (1905–1908), he mentions Alberic. There is nostalgia and pain, but no sign of moroseness in his correspondence. Pierre speaks of the passing of his brother with deep feeling and tenderness, as if this death had a direct and lasting effect upon his life. Instead of diminishing with time, his memories seem only to increase with fondness and depth during his years of theology at Hastings (1908–1912).

Just who was Alberic for Teilhard? Alberic embodied for him the ideal older brother: handsome, intelligent, courageous, the type of man that the younger Pierre spontaneously desired to imitate. He was a unique model of that consistency which Teilhard so craved. But alas! At the very apex of his manhood, Alberic was struck by a slow and pitiful emaciation that ended in death.

Such a soul-wrenching experience in Pierre's impressionable youth must have shattered a host of idols within his world. At the age of twenty-one, on the occasion of this heartrending ordeal, he was forced to face with particular acuity these critical questions of life: What is death? Does it have a positive meaning? Does incorruptibility exist even where we are apparently most corruptible?

A meditative reflection on the death of Alberic in its relation to the interior maturation of Teilhard helps us to appreciate a little more the following sentiments addressed to Marguerite in 1916: "I really liked Blondel's lines on suffering which you sent me. Through every word shone the creative, formative action of God whose influence alone has the power to detach us from ourselves. . . . That is precisely what makes the passivities of existence seem so delicate and worthy of adoration since through them God asserts his primacy over us. . . . The more I think of it, the more I find that death, by the great invasion and intrusion of everything new that it represents in our individual development, is a liberation and a solace—even in spite of the fact that it is essentially painful (because it is essentially regenerating and detaching)."[8]

The death of Alberic as well as the passing away of others whom he loved so much both within and outside the family certainly constitute painful intrusions upon his individual development. These intrusions are without him, in spite of him. Yet, beyond their appearances these detachments efficaciously bear witness to the creative, formative influence of God: an influence which detaches him, freeing and regenerating him in God.

B. A Dead End: The Cult of Inert Passivities

In the letter to Marguerite cited above, Teilhard had introduced his remarks regarding the passivities of existence by referring to his "cult" of them. By cult in this context he means an attitude of joyous, voluntary submission arising from personal conviction. This he distinguishes vigorously from the "cult of passivity" which he sees so prevalent in Oriental mysticism. The cult of passivity consists in succumbing to "the temptation of matter" (small "m"), thus giving in to the inclination towards least effort. This latter is a false cult wrongly pursued by certain putative mystics, especially those favoring a pantheism of fusion and dissolution.[9]

Teilhard knows by personal experience whereof he speaks, for he found himself locked into *a dead end (un point mort)* in this regard. It came about this way: Teilhard had grown up in a familial and religious milieu which was staunchly dualistic and thoroughly imbued with Jansenism. There was his Christian self and his pagan self; his love of God and his love of the World. He wanted desperately to dedicate his service both to the Church and to science. The same passion was going in two apparently irreconcilable directions at the same time. He firmly believed that they could be—indeed, must be—capable of being integrated, but he was powerless to do so himself. Nor could he find much help in seeking spiritual guidance other than the sound advice that somehow he must continue to pursue both as far as they might take him.

In his late twenties, Teilhard became deeply frustrated with the inability of the asceticism in which he had been reared to bring about a peaceful resolution of this seemingly interminable, interior conflict. So, without clearly adverting to what was happening during his regency in Egypt (1905–1908), he began to drift further and further into the cult of inert passivity. This cult consisted in a sliding back and down into the multiple (scatteredness, dissipation), rather than struggling forward and upward towards true union in love.

"In order to be All, I must be fused with all. . . . Such was the mystical movement to which, following so many Hindu poets and mystics, I was logically being driven by an innate, ungovernable need to attain self-fulfillment. . . by becoming one with the Other." Teilhard might really have succumbed to this temptation "had it not been that just in the nick of time the idea of Evolution sprouted up within me, like a seed: whence it came I cannot say."[10]

Thus, it was actually the notion of Evolution—ultimately that of Christogenesis—which constituted the resolution of his interior dilemma. Like a presence welling up within him, the realization came to Teilhard that the detachment inherent in the process of transforming union is not a question of Matter *versus* Spirit, nor even of Matter *and* Spirit, but rather of Matter *becoming* Spirit. Spirit is that which being is becoming. In this way, spiritualization is not accomplished by dematerializing oneself, but instead by letting Christ christify one's self, by letting his Spirit spiritualize one's Matter (Rom. 7–8; 1 Cor. 15). This truth is at the core of the passivities of existence. This is what makes them so worthy of adoration. This is authentic Christian receptivity.

72

In *The Road of the West: Towards a New Mysticism* (1932) as well as in other essays,[11] Teilhard contrasts Oriental mysticism with Christian mysticism. Using terminology common to both, he describes mysticism in general as the teaching and the practice of attaining both the Universal and the Spiritual simultaneously and through each other. Thus, at the same time and by the same act, we become one with the All *(Todo)* by a Power abiding within us, but which is not of us. This Power (i.e., the transforming activity of God) frees us from multiplicity, scatteredness and dissipation. In this manner, the mystic attains all things in God in their ultimate degree of purification and transformation.

The *Road of the East* is characterized by a movement towards spiritual union through return to a common divine basis. This élan would attain oneness by suppression of the multiple (hence, by negation and withdrawal) and by retreating from the interior forward propensity of evolutionary effort towards individuation and personalization. Thus, absorption of self into the mass would replace differentiation of self and of others. Oriental mysticism is a pantheism of identification in which one becomes coextensive with the sphere through dissolution of self and others. Everything and everyone are engulfed in one huge mass. The human person would then exist in a complacent rest which would be the result of withdrawal from the tension inherent in straining forward.

The *Road of the West,* on the other hand, is characterized by a movement towards spiritual union through convergence forward *(en Avant)* and upward *(en Haut)* towards the ultimate point of consummation, the Omega Point. This is accomplished by becoming one with the All through consummate differentiation of self and by convergence with all other persons and things in Christ. "True union ascending towards Spirit is accomplished by establishing in their own perfection the elements which it dominates. Union differentiates."[12] Thus, there is a sense in which the term "pantheism" may be applied to Christian mysticism: "God all in all" (1 Cor. 15:28; Eph. 1:23; Col. 1:19). This refers to transforming union with God in love and in him with all creation. Unification transpires by concentration and transformation at the Center of the Sphere, together with sublimation and metamorphosis of Matter and of the Multiple in the Spirit. In this way, a very real tension and restlessness (Rom. 8:24–25; Phil. 3:13–14) are necessarily integral to the whole process of transforming love.

Thus, in his search for true Consistency and in his quest to be united with Truth, Teilhard was tempted to indulge in the cult of false passivity. He was saved, however, by a true passivity: the intervention of a force, a new light which sprang forth from within him permeating his interior like a Presence. This influence within him, yet not of him, manifested itself in proportion to his own effort: the spiritual effort of receptivity to Truth, of letting himself be corrected, of letting himself be reformed by the creative, formative action of God.

In this way, the dead end of the pantheism of fusion and dissolution did not cause a lapse into nothing-nothingness (which is certainly not the *nada* of St. John of the Cross). Rather it worked like a catalyst prodding Teilhard to encounter grace (which is indeed true *nada*). This grace did not arise from the dead end as such. It emanated from God. But it was manifested through this temptation even though the source of the grace was beyond it. God does not tempt the soul. This is entirely a question of a temptation of matter. God exercises the soul. He tests it, and causes it to pass on.

In this way, God used this situation to teach Teilhard an invaluable lesson: namely, the One who seeks him and whom he seeks can never be found in the direction of matter, but only in the direction of Spirit. In fact, "the sense of Plenitude was turned upside down in me. And I have followed this new direction ever since without ever looking back. . . . It literally spun me around in my fundamental quest for Consistency."[13]

The death of Alberic and the ordeal of the temptation of

matter constituted painful, salutary experiences which Teilhard underwent in faith. Through them, God asserted his primacy over him, and deepened his search for the Absolute. However, the passivity of existence which was perhaps the most detaching (at least up to the age of thirty-six) occurred during his involvement in the battle of Verdun.

2. Teilhard's Interior Crisis of May–June 1916

At this period of his life Teilhard was corresponding with his cousin Marguerite two or three times a week and writing in his *Journal* almost daily. Then, all of a sudden, we discover complete silence with regard to both. There are no letters to Marguerite between April 9 and June 18 and no entries in his *Journal* from May 14 to June 26. Consequently, we possess no direct references concerning the conflict which was coming to a head within him. However, immediately after passing through the most intense part of the trial, Teilhard does name certain specific elements of his interior crisis.[14]

A first aspect he calls a "sort of numbness," a certain personal difficulty with regard to his military duties. Teilhard was a stretcher-bearer for an infantry regiment. "I've been very down of late. I don't seem to be able to muster any effort. . . . Perhaps it is something physical, a kind of lethargy that is making me so listless. One thing though is sure: my natural energies have been depleted. I'm near exhaustion." To Marguerite he confesses: "I no longer feel like myself: the individual monad full of plans for personal activity. Rather I feel lost in this gigantic clash of nations and brutal energies. This has left me drained and depersonalized."

A second dimension to his trial is linked intimately with the first: Christ seems hidden from him. "Add to this my being deprived of the celebration of the Eucharist. This is somewhat compensated for, since I am carrying the Blessed Sacrament on me."

Yet, this privation pierced through to the very core of his being: "How distant Our Lord seems to me now!"

Reflecting on Teilhard's pain, one cannot but recall the lines of the opening stanza of the *Spiritual Canticle*: "Where have you hidden youself, oh my Beloved, and have left me in anguish. . . . I went out searching frantically for you, and you were gone."

Teilhard indicates two other characteristics of his crisis in this prayer which he addresses to Jesus: "My soul is weighed down and unsettled. My mind and my heart are captivated by ideals which I sometimes fear may be neither heavenly enough nor sufficiently orthodox. O Master, preserve in me and in those whom I love so much—whatever the cost!—the light of your purity and of your truth."

Teilhard's prayer regarding his heart and purity is in reference to his vow of celibacy. A glance at his *Journal* entries immediately preceding this event reveals just how preoccupied he was with sexuality and chastity: February 8, 10, 14, 20; March 9, 12; April 27, 29; May 3–6, 8–10, (1916). He was certainly struggling in his effort to integrate his love for a particular woman with his commitment to Christ.

Teilhard's prayer regarding his mind and truth is in reference to the intense conflict arising within him between certain cries of unorthodoxy coming from some of his confreres and the authenticity of what he considered to be a personal charism: the reconciliation of God and the World. Or, as he was to put it the following year: "My vocation is to be the apostle of the Communion with God through the Cosmos."[15]

Of the three trials which St. John of the Cross singles out as most characteristic of the deepest throes of the night of sense—spirit of fornication, spirit of blasphemy and spirit of dizziness[16]—Teilhard gives indication of having undergone all three. The spirit of fornication: his struggle with his consecrated celibacy and chastity. The spirit of blasphemy: his questioning God for depriving him of Mass and for seeming to be so far away. The spirit of dizziness: doubts about his own orthodoxy and personal charism—fears, scruples, perplexities for which he can find no solution.

Teilhard reveals still another aspect of this crisis of May–June 1916: "What has been going on in me this month is a loss of my will to live. The very source of my strength has gone out from me. 'If salt becomes insipid, how can it be made salty again [Matt. 5:13]?' In a very real sense I seem to have lost all confidence and interest in myself."

In this condition he asks himself what should be his proper interior attitude: "What is one to do in this case where one can find no support of any kind? I must cling fast to Our Lord without feeling anything, and pray. . . . For if I succeed in doing this, what joy and peace I will discover in humbling myself without limit before Our Lord, in losing myself by letting go all confidence in myself. . . until I am completely united with his divine will!"

On the feast of the Sacred Heart (June 30 that year), Teilhard synthesized for himself the various elements of this trial as well as their profound meaning: "I can see more clearly now what was so disconcerting for me at Verdun. It was the concrete and immediate sight of possible destruction." He really believed that he would be killed. "I experienced in every fiber of my being what it means to be utterly lost, and to have to give up every cherished hope, every meaningful plan. . . . This threat overshadowed me, chilling and freezing in some way all my ardor. My will to live and to act was wiped out. . . . The sources of my life withered." He prays: "Jesus, grant me true, sincere and courageous renunciation founded on absolute faith in him who is stronger than death" (Song of Sol. 8:6; Phil. 3:9). Teilhard concludes: "The heart of Our Lord is the source of all the passivities which exert mastery over me and of all the activities which awaken me and sweep me along."[17]

Two years later, Teilhard expressed the above conclusion in

a formula which became very dear to him: *"Quidquid patimur, Christum patimur"* (Whatever we suffer, we suffer Christ). *"Quidquid agimus, Christus agitur"* (Whatever we do, Christ is done).[18] In effect, these complementary aspects of the mystery of Christ in our personal, daily lives constitute the principal subject matter of *The Divine Milieu* (1927).

The events of May–June 1916 are among the most significant in the interior genesis of Teilhard de Chardin. Before attaining this breakthrough, he underwent a long and painstaking maturation under God's guidance. This spiritual threshold constitutes for him a real personal conversion, a veritable fundamental option, a true spiritual death and resurrection. It was as if the old Teilhard had died somewhere in the wild countryside near Verdun in order to allow the new Teilhard to be reborn out of the depths of human despair. Four months later, as a matter of fact, he composed *Christ in Matter* (October 1916) to capture the significance of those events. This essay comprises three stories in the style of Robert Hugh Benson, a very symbolic and unique literary form for Teilhard. The first story—that of the picture of the Sacred Heart—recaptures his thirty-five years of struggle to see the reconciliation of Christ and Matter. The second account—that of the monstrance—expresses the intensely transforming and purifying events of May–June 1916. The third story—that of the pyx—brings out the realization that even though a fundamental breakthrough had been accomplished, there still remained a barrier between Christ and himself. That barrier consisted of all the years and of all that he had yet to do and to suffer before his death.[19]

With these passivities in mind, we appreciate all the more those poignant lines he wrote to Marguerite on December 18, 1916: "I remain faithful to my cult of the other component of the Real: that is, to the powerful energies which force our staunchest resistances to bend before them and acknowledge their mastery. I really liked Blondel's lines on suffering which you sent me.

Through every word shone the creative, formative action of God whose influence alone has the power to detach us from ourselves 'in order to place in us something that is not of us'—'Oh, the joy of experiencing the action of the Other within us!' That is precisely what makes the passivities of existence seem so delicate and so worthy of adoration (since through them God asserts his primacy over us)." Teilhard concludes: "The more I think of it, the more I find that death, by the great invasion and intrusion of everything new that it represents in our individual development, is a liberation and a solace—even in spite of the fact that it is essentially painful (because it is essentially regenerating and detaching)."

3. Promoting the Passivities of Existence

What must be not only our attitude towards, but also our voluntary collaboration with, all that we undergo throughout life? Teilhard responds: "I do not give way passively to these blessed passivities, Lord. Rather, I offer myself actively to them, and I do all in my power to promote them."[20]

We can understand without too much difficulty what is meant by offering ourselves to these passivities. It means to be open to them, to leave ourselves open before them, and above all to let ourselves be opened by them. It means persisting in an attitude of true Christian resignation which invites and promotes the action of the Other in us. This resignation is active in two senses: (1) Together with God we must energetically resist evil. And (2) true abandonment to God is itself a positive and affirmative act on our part. We must say "yes" to these passivities and honestly mean it. Therefore, if we are really to commune with God operating within us and all around us, it is not enough to simply let come what may, but we must positively give ourselves to him who comes in and through the very act of receptivity.

Teilhard explains: "My God, in order to promote and foster your activity within me through all things, I must do even more than open myself and offer myself to the passivities of existence. I must voluntarily associate myself with the work you effect in my body and in my soul. I must strive to obey and to anticipate your slightest impulses. My cherished wish, O Lord, is that I might offer so little resistance to you that you could no longer distinguish me from yourself—so perfectly would we be united in the communion of one Will!"[21]

We must offer ourselves and remain receptive even to the point of striving to obey and anticipate the least promptings of the divine Presence within us. This is what is meant by not giving way to them passively, in the sense of inert passivity. It is necessary to make the effort—the terribly demanding spiritual effort—of being and of remaining Christianly passive, receptive.[22] The mystical act par excellence is that of unreserved, passionate abandonment of the soul in sheer faith to ineffable Love: the *no-sé-qué*.[23] This personal, spiritual effort; this total, passionate surrender; this positive resignation constitute the apex of our voluntary cooperation with the transforming and purifying activity of God within us. This is the quality and the intensity of receptivity that Teilhard designates by the expression, "promoting and fostering the passivities of existence."

However, this receptivity, as comprehensive and intense as it may be, still does not exhaust all the positive richness of our collaboration with Christ. The complete offering of self to God attains its fullness only when accompanied by a maximum personal effort to collaborate actively in producing the best possible *opus* (work, labor, task, product). In the faithful accomplishment of our daily chores—even down to the most minute details—we bring to Christ a little more fulfillment. Thus, we not only make up for what is lacking in the passion of Christ (Col. 1:24), but we also contribute our share in making up what is lacking in his activity.[24]

By both receptivity and activity then, we do our best qualitatively and quantitatively to promote as fully as possible the creative, formative action of God within us and around us. In this twofold way, we contribute positively to the transformation of all things through him, with him, in him. For in whatever we suffer, undergo, endure, we receive Christ. And in whatever we do, foster, promote—not only in terms of good intention *(operatio)*, but also down to the most material aspect of the activity *(opus)*—we collaborate with Christ in building up his Body.

Teilhard perceives activity as related to the passivities of existence in four complementary ways. First, the power to act is itself gratuitously received in the primordial gift of existence: "What do you have [what are you] that you have not received?" (1 Cor. 4:7). The very first passivity for each person is his/her gift of being-becoming. This is the very first fruit of the Spirit (Rom. 8:23). Second, maximum effort and maximum fidelity in every undertaking serve as an essential sign of authenticity regarding true receptivity. This effort prunes and discerns authentic passivities from lassitude, laziness and the temptation of matter. Third, the daily accomplishment of one's tasks with uncompromising honesty and fidelity for Christ constitutes a formidable asceticism. Detachment through action! If I really do exactly what God wants of me minute-by-minute, hour-by-hour—as his providence reveals it to me through all the converging circumstances of the moment—then he will purge me of self-centeredness through my fidelity to this activity. Fourth, an active and vigorous resistance against all evil is necessary in order to arrive at true Christian resignation.[25]

Our considerations in this chapter pertain to the passivities of existence, of life, of just living, being, becoming. After World War I, however, Teilhard ceases using the expression "passivities of existence" in preference for a more precise designation based on the perspective of the person receiving them. Henceforth he distinguishes the passivities of growth and the passivities of diminishment.

Notes from Chapter 3

1. *MM*, Dec. 28, 1916, pp. 156–158. (The same for the quotations which follow.)
2. *Writings*, p. 139.
3. *HM*, pp. 196–208.
4. *HM*, pp. 15–17. The French word *sens* means both "sense" or intuition (as in sense of mystery) and "direction" (as in *sens unique*: one-way street). Teilhard intends both senses.
5. *HM*, pp.. 17–29, 197–198.
6. *HM*, pp. 29–58, 82–99, 199–208.
7. *HM*, pp. 17-44; 197.
8. *MM*, Dec. 28, 1916, p. 158.
9. *HM*, pp. 23–24; *CE*, pp. 56–75.
10. *HM*, pp. 24–29, 45–49.
11. *TF*, pp. 40–59. 134–147, 199–205, 209–211, etc.
12. *HE*, p. 144.
13. *HM*, pp. 26–28.
14. The following quotations are taken from his *Journal*, June 26–30, 1916, and from *MM*, pp. 100–101 (letter of June 18, 1916).
15. *Journal*, Dec. 22, 1917.
16. *Night*, I, 14, 2–3. See *Contemplation*, p. 85–96.
17. *Journal*, June 30, 1916. See *MM*, pp. 106–108.
18. *Writings*, p. 259; *Journal*, Feb. 28, 1919; *HM*, p. 204; *DM*, p. 123.
19. *HU*, pp. 41–55; *HM*, pp. 61–67.
20. "The Priest" (1918), in *Writings*, p. 215.
21. *Writing*, p. 216.
22. "There is nothing more crucifying. . . . than spiritual effort" (*SC*, p. 69).
23. The "I-don't-know-what" *(Canticle,* stanza 7).
24. *DM*, pp. 49–62.
25. *DM*, pp. 62–73, 90–93.

Chapter 4

Passivities of Growth and of Diminishment

Teilhard composed his first book, *The Divine Milieu* (1927), to serve as testimony to his deepest convictions regarding the spiritual life. He dedicated it to those who love the World, since God has so loved the World (John 3:16). This book comprises three sections: (1) the divinization of our activities, (2) the divinization of our passivities, and (3) the Divine Milieu proper. *Les passivités de croissance* and *les passivités de diminution* constitute the subject matter of the second section.[1]

1. Human Passivities in General

After a lengthly development of our powers, energies and capacities, we eventually arrive at the stark recognition of the influence of passivities within our lives. Little by little we become conscious that we receive immeasurably more than we give, and we gradually realize that we are dominated by the objects of our conquests. "Like Jacob wrestling with the angel, the soul faithful to life and to grace ends up by adoring the One whom it was struggling against" (Gen. 32:26–31).

Paradoxically, "the soul has hardly arrived at the heart of things, when it finds itself ready to be detached from them. Having taken its fill of the Universe and of itself, the soul one day discovers that it is possessed by an intense need to die to self and to be led beyond itself. Moreover, this is not the result of disillusionment, but rather issues forth as a logical development of its own effort."[2] One cannot but see the baptismal symbol underlying the truth which Teilhard is expressing: namely, that immersion in the World with Christ, which is the first phase of our incorporation in him, is necessarily followed by a second phase, that of our emergence from the World in Christ. Or, to paraphrase John the Baptizer: initially I must increase so that Christ may increase, but eventually I must decrease so that he can further increase (John 3:30).

Immersion and emergence are like breathing in and breathing out; like the arsis and thesis of a musical measure. The more you take in, the more you let out (let go); the greater the upbeat, the more meaningful the downbeat. That is, the more realistic is our incarnation in the World with Christ, the more complete is our renunciation of the World for him. These are not two movements, but one movement in two phases. Each phase is characterized by its own type of receptivity. The passivities of growth pertain mainly to the sphere of immersion, whereas the passivities of diminishment are associated principally with emergence. As a matter of fact, our activities are sandwiched in between these two genres of passivities. We receive the ability to act. We then activate that capacity, which activity leads us ultimately to total abandonment to God in love.

In its most general sense, therefore, the term "passivities" refers to everything that is received by and within the human person. What is not done by us, is by definition undergone in us. Thus, our passivities embrace the immense complex of every-

84

thing within us and around us, without us and in spite of us. This complex is as vast, as intricate and as incomprehensible as the totality of the World's past and present.

From the point of view of the person receiving these passivities, we distinguish two groups. Our destination stems from our surface perception of them as being amicable or painful to us. Those friendly and favorable forces that sustain our effort and point the way towards what we ordinarily consider success, we call passivities of growth. Those hostile powers which laboriously obstruct our innate tendencies, hampering or impeding what we normally consider progress towards heightened being are termed passivities of diminishment.

2. Passivities of Growth

"We undergo Life at least as much as, if not more than, we undergo Death."

This truth eventually impresses itself upon the consciousness of every thinking person. Living and dying—are they something we do, or are they done to us? In their most profound sense, both life and death are actively received in us, by us. Obviously they are primarily passive. Yet there is surely something we must do about each of them. In the case of life, we have to correspond to it, cooperate with it. Otherwise the gift is squandered. In the case of death, we must accept it, become resigned to God through it and beyond it. Not only do we have to say *amen*, but we must especially be *amen*.

So natural to us are living and growing that we do not usually pause long enough to distinguish our activities from the host of passivities which nourish that action or from the given circumstances which favor its success. Generally we take for granted our health, our self, our life, until of course something happens: illness, contradiction, death.

How, then, do we get in touch with this immense wealth of

reality which Teilhard calls our passivities of growth? We must penetrate prayerfully the depths of our most elusive selves and there try to perceive the ocean of forces to which we are subjected and in which our personal as well as collective development is steeped. We have to enter into ourselves in deepest recollection to imbibe the depth and universality of our dependence on so much which remains altogether outside our control and which goes to make up the intimacy of our communion with the World to which we belong.

So, with the light of faith and intuition, I leave behind the zone of everyday preoccupations and relationships where everything has a name and a place and a number, to search and to listen with my heart to those depths whence I feel dimly that my power of action emanates. But as I move further and further away from the conventional certainties on which social life thrives, I discover that I am losing contact with myself. At each step of the descent a new aspect of person is disclosed within me, the name of which I am no longer certain and which no longer obeys me. And, when I stop my exploration because the path fades from beneath my steps, I find a fathomless abyss at my feet, out of which comes—I know not whence—the stream which I dare call *my* life. My life: *vita mea!* My life is not really mine *(mei)* as if it were of me, rather it is to me *(mihi)*. What is mine that I have not received (1 Cor. 4:7)?

What human endeavor will ever be able to reveal to me the unfathomable origins of my being? Certainly not my own effort or that of anyone else around me. Nor can I or anyone else effectively change who I truly am and who I am truly becoming. Oh, I may be able of course to trace my roots back several generations. By means of certain ascetical and physical disciplines, I might even stabilize or enlarge certain aspects of my ability to receive. But none of these can harness the deepest sources of life. "My self is given to me far more than it is formed by me." My destiny is shaped within me far more than I shape it. "In the ultimate analysis the interior life, life at its source, the nascent life completely eludes our grasp."

That is the firstfruit of my interior journey to discover the passivities of growth. The second flows from the first. Shaken by this realization, I want to return to the light of day and forget this disturbing enigma in comfortable surroundings and familiar things. This temptation of matter would have me forsake my salutary quest and settle instead for lassitude, complacency and mediocrity. But just when I am about to succumb, there—beyond all this darkness and confusion—appears the Unknown, the I-don't-know-what, that I am trying to escape. It (he!) is not only deeper than the abyss, but also intimately intertwined among the innumerable strands of the web of providence: the very stuff of which the universe and my own individuality are woven. He infinitely transcends my life and my world, yet he remains the immanent, vital force not only at the Alpha and Omega of my being, but also all the way through my becoming.

A third effect also results from my interior journey to search out the passivities of growth. The third flows from the first and the second. I begin to reel even more when I try to contemplate, much less number, the myriad of favorable influences which must have converged to produce me. I could go out of my mind trying to analyze the supreme improbability, the incalculable unlikelihood of finding myself existing at all in a world that has actually survived and succeeded in being a world. Thus, having come to the realization that my life is not really mine, but to me, and that I am called infinitely beyond myself, I discover the indescribable poverty of my spirit and the ultimate meaning of the first beatitude: Blessed are those who know their true need, for God is theirs and they are God's (Matt. 5:3).

But there is still a fourth dimension of my interior journey. The fourth recapitulates the previous three. As anyone else will find who dares make the same pilgrimage, I felt the anxiety characteristic of a person lost, adrift, floundering, when I encountered the fathomlessness of my own personhood, the utter transcendency of the God for whom my soul pines and the seeming endlessness of my inner poverty. And, if something—Someone— saved me from my distress, it was the gentle and unmistakable voice of Jesus coming across the lake and "from out of the depth of the night: 'I am. Be not afraid' " (John 6:20). Faith in the Son of God is the culminating effect of my quest to encounter the passivities of growth.

This faith, however, must be translated into daily life, into actual attitudes and action. In the Life that wells up in me (John 4:14) and in the Matter which sustains me, I find much more than God's gift. I encounter God himself: he who makes me participate in his being and molds me in his likeness (2 Cor. 3:18). I discover, as it were, the two hands of the Father. One hand holds me so firmly, yet so tenderly, that it coincides with all the sources of my life. In it I experience the Father's immanence. His other hand stretches beyond my wildest imagination in all-embracive coherence, holding together the immensity of the cosmos. In it I encounter his omnipresence, his transcendence.

We must respond to this discovery in twofold fashion: on the one hand, by our personal will to be and to become more and more; and on the other hand, by making our contribution to the being and ultimate becoming of all the created realities which providence brings into our lives. That is, we must take care, first of all, that we never stifle, distort or waste our power to love, to do or to become. Then, we must strive never to miss an opportunity to direct others towards Spirit.

The life of each of us is woven of these two threads. There is the thread of interior development and the thread of outward achievement: our within *(le dedans)* and our without *(le dehors)*. In the former are gradually molded our ideas, our affections, our human and religious attitudes. In the latter "we always find ourselves at the exact point where the whole sum of the energies of the universe converge to effect in us the work which God desires."

"May I never break this double thread of my life."

3. Passivities of Diminishment

To be open to God within the internal and external forces which animate our being and sustain its development means basically to be open to and to trust all the influences of life. In responding to the passivities of growth by our fidelilty to action, we commune with God. Thus, the desire to undergo God leads us to the very fulfilling task of promoting our own personal growth and that of others.

However, "the soul faithful to Life and to Grace cannot proceed indefinitely in the direction of building up a strong self. . . . It gradually becomes aware of the emergence from the very operation of its impulse toward self-fulfillment of a hostile component that grows more dominant: the predilection for renunciation."[3]

How amazing! The zest for being and the quest for the fullness of life have within their own inner dynamics the predilection for detachment, for death to self. Moreover, this is a logical and necessary outcome of this development. All true growth, all real development—in short, all Progress towards Spirit, towards the qualitative, towards the interior—is accomplished ultimately only through a *metanoia* (conversion): "The World cannot attain consummate fulfillment except through a death, a 'night.'. . . . The Earth does not take cognizance of its destiny except through the crisis of a conversion."[4]

To encounter God as the animator of the passivities of growth is truly awesome. It is terrifying, freeing and hope-filled—all at the same time. But what is this predilection for renunciation? We can understand something of the meaning of the zest for life, the zest for being and becoming. But how can anyone develop a taste for detachment? The fact that God is discovered in and through life we readily accept. But can God be found not only also, but above all in and through death? And yet, the incontestable lesson of every living creature and of all interior progress has always been that one must die in order to rise transformed: "Unless the

89

grain of wheat falls into the ground and dies. . . . " (John 12:24–25). Resurrection not only follows death, in the sense of coming after it, but resurrection occurs especially in death, through it and out of it.

The passivities of growth develop us. These friendly and favorable forces which sustain our effort and direct us towards Progress really foster growth. Nonetheless, in an extremely paradoxical manner the passivities of diminishment cause us to grow even more. These hostile powers which in one way reduce and even destroy our capacities for development constitute in another way the passivities par excellence by which we commune with God. Of all the passivities we are subject to in this life, the passivities of diminishment remain those most charged with power to divinize.

The expressions "of growth" and "of diminishment" designate, then, a division of the passivities of existence into two general categories. These qualifying words denote that aspect which at first sight strikes the observer. Some passivities appear friendly, others seem hostile. However, beyond their appearances both genres exercise a truly positive and interacting influence on our interior progress: "Even though physically we may be falling into decay, our inner selves are being renewed day by day" (2 Cor. 4:16).

How is this possible? The response of Teilhard is that of St. Paul: "For those who love God, everything is transformed into good" (Rom. 8:28). And they do mean absolutely everything (Rom. 8:31–39).

"The forces of diminishment are, nonetheless, our real passivities," for not only do we suffer them, but also we suffer immensely from them. "The ways they affect us are innumerable, their forms infinitely varied, their influence constant. In order to understand them better, we shall divide them into two groups. . . those diminishments which originate within us and those which originate outside us."

Generally speaking, the external passivities of diminishment comprise all our experiences of ill fortune. They spring up from all sides. They may be the microbe which infects the body or the inopportune word that wounds the heart. They are the incidents and the accidents of varying importance and diverse kinds which crush us, hurt us, anger and frustrate us. They are the barriers that block our way, the walls that hem us in, the defeats that bring us down.

All these passivities are diminishing enough, but the ones whose origin is within us "constitute the darkest element and the most despairingly useless years of our lives." They are represented by all kinds of natural defects. They are all the physical, intellectual and moral limitations that plague us, restrict us, humiliate us from birth to death. They are the temperamental, nervous, personality and emotional disorders which overtake us all sooner or later, one way or another. They are our moodiness, our sinfulness, our innumerable manifestations of selfishness. In the end, old age itself gradually robs us of all vigor, pushing us irreversibly towards death. Even the passage of time *(la durée)* is a formidable passivity. It is either too long or too short. It is either too cluttered or too empty, too much or not enough. But in any case it moves us inevitably towards death.

Death. "Death is the apex and the consummation of all our diminishments. Death is the epitome itself of all evil." It epitomizes physical evil inasmuch as it results organically from the complete disintegration of matter to which we are all subject. It epitomizes moral evil inasmuch as it is immeasurably compounded by the abuse of freedom and by the sin of the world (John 1:29). Yet, death surrenders us totally to God. Through it we pass over to him by losing ourselves in Someone greater than ourselves.

Thus, death is also supreme good. But how? How can that which is the epitome of evil *(le Mal)* be transformed into the greatest good?

A. The Struggle with God against Evil

The first question that must be posed regarding the transformation of evil into good is this: Just what is the relationship of God to evil? In response to this question, we shall summarize the points of view (1) of the scholastics, (2) of St. John of the Cross and (3) of Teilhard.

(1) The classical scholastic view is formulated according to these distinctions: God wills good directly. He wills physical evil only indirectly. He merely permits moral evil.

(2) The Sanjuanist perspective introduces into this tripartite framework certain subtle nuances. Even during the most trying temptations of the night of sense, the influence of God within us remains constant and positive. In fact, it is the loving, transforming activity of God in direct contact with our inner poverty that produces all the pain and darkness which John calls night. God himself sends these storms and trials in order that, having been chastised and buffeted, we may advance more securely in our search for absolute good. These storms exercise us, disposing us and accommodating our senses and faculties for union with God in love. "If the soul is not tempted, exercised and proved by these trials and temptations, its senses cannot be strengthened in preparation for Wisdom."[5] Even Jesus "was led by the Spirit out into the desert in order to be tempted" (Matt. 4:1).

(3) Teilhard adds a complementary insight to the two preceding views. When suffering befalls him/her, the Christian says with Job (19:21), "The Lord has touched me." This, of course, is profoundly true. But, this affirmation, so tersely formulated, summarizes a whole complex of influences: some very good and divine, others very evil and painful. Thus, only when we have passed all the way through these influences, do those words attain their full truth.

If we retrace the beginning of our encounters with a given evil situation, we realize that we prayed at that moment—and continually thereafter—as did Jesus in Gethsemane (Luke 22:41–44): Lord, free me from this diminishment. I want with all my being to assist you in removing this chalice from me. However, not my will, but yours be done!

These words express the first will, so to speak, of our Father: namely, that every evil—even physical evil—be reduced to a minimum. Indeed, the Father wills that it be done away with entirely whenever possible. The Father wants each of us to struggle together with him against every evil. Therefore, at the approach of these diminishments, we are called upon to utilize all our resources in order to struggle against whatever is of evil in them. This resistance is absolutely necessary if we are to adhere as faithfully as possible to the creative action of God within us and all around us.

However, even if we wrestle with God against evil, despite all our effort we shall sooner or later be vanquished by evil. For, in the end, each one of us must die. How, then, do we find God's will in this? What is the significance of defeat?

B. Our Apparent Defeat and Its Transformation

The problem of evil—that is, the reconciliation of our failures with the creative goodness and power of God—remains one of the most disturbing mysteries of the universe for both our hearts and our minds. This is all the more perplexing when we read in the Gospel "that it is necessary for scandal to occur" (Matt. 18:7). It is difficult enough to have to admit that failure, sin and death do exist. But what is really difficult to admit is that they *must* exist.

Teilhard responds to this enigma in several ways, all of which converge in one manner or another on the providence of God in the actual economy of salvation. He does not indulge in "what-if's" or in "what-might-have-been's."

A first response stems from the evolutionary process itself.

93

Everything that becomes suffers and commits its own faults. One cannot get through the first of the three phases of the dialectic of evolution (divergence, convergence, emergence) without experiencing many blind alleys, dead-ends and explorations incompatible with self-fulfillment. In the ultimate analysis, we all learn and grow by experience. And experience is gained only at the price of much suffering, failure and after many mistakes. Just ask the son of the prodigal father (Luke 15:13–17). In every aspect of evolution there is both continuity and discontinuity. In the process of becoming, something endures and something is necessarily left behind. At every step of the way something must be relinquished. Advancement always costs. Nature abounds with examples: the grain of wheat, the caterpillar, the cutting of the apron strings, etc.

A second response flows from the nature of evolution, especially as directed toward a point of ultimate consummation. Evolution (or genesis) is movement from the imperfect to the perfect. It is transition from scatteredness to unification. Evolution is transformation from chaos to accomplished being. This necessitates intense struggle, both interior and exterior. One cannot succeed in becoming more without exerting immense effort at considerable cost of energy and discipline. We have only to think of the endeavors of athletes, scholars and diplomats.

A third response views the laws of statistical necessity latent within evolution. Within the universe there is such a multitude of agents pursuing their own individual and collective progress that some of these energies are bound not only to cross, but to clash head-on. Most of the cycles of nature are predicated upon this principle. What is good for one species is death to another. What is meal for the fox is end for the rabbit. Thus, plants drain minerals from the soil, cattle eat the plants, humans dine on beef, and then they in turn fertilize the ground. Other examples related to the laws of statistical necessity can be given: traffic fatality predictions for the Labor Day weekend, Murphy's Law (whatever can go wrong will sooner or later), etc.

A fourth response considers the inner nature of created being becoming. Within creation as a whole and within each individual creature in particular, there exist two contrary forces: entropy and evolution. Entropy is that innate tendency which turns the creature in upon itself, whereas evolution, especially in the Teilhardian sense of genesis, is that energy within each being driving it beyond its present state to become something more. Translated into the realm of human beings (the Noosphere), entropy becomes self-centeredness, pride, sin; whereas evolution elicits gift of self, commitment, love.

When we understand the above four responses specifically in the light of the Christ-event, the necessity of suffering and death assumes a new significance and a decidedly positive thrust. Not only are we called to become fully human, but also to participate in the very life of God himself, to be united to him in love through transforming union. Thus, "if being united means in every case migrating and dying at least partially in/to what one loves, then this being annihilated in the other must be all the more complete the more we give our attachment to the One who is greater than ourselves. We can set no limits to the uprooting that is involved in our journey in God."

But the myopic person still counters: Couldn't God have made a better world? A universe without pain, failure, death? A journey that would be easier, simpler, more enjoyable? This narcissistic view of the world perceives the cost of progress as good or bad inasmuch as it suits or does not suit one's own likes and dislikes.

Yet, even transcending a self-centered appraisal of divine providence, we can see it at best only upside down and in reverse, as if we were looking at the underneath portion of a tapestry. All we see are loose ends and disjointed patterns. Instead, we must view the world and our lives in faith, from God's loving perspective: looking down from above, as it were. For God did indeed make the best possible world according to his purpose, which is transforming union.

Thus, our defeat only appears as such. We merely seem to fail. In view of Jesus's paschal mystery, no effort is ever wasted, no struggle is ever in vain, no death is without some victory. Everything is transformed into good for those who believe in him (Rom. 8:28). This good may not be apparent to the victim: for example, to the soldier who falls during the assault which leads to peace. Nevertheless, God does bring forth not only some good, but a greater good. He produces something greater than what would otherwise have been. "Like the artist who knows how to use a flaw in the rock he sculptures in order to bring out more exquisite lines, God—provided we abandon ourselves to him in faith and love—transforms everything into our good. For those who seek God, not everything is immediately good, but everything is capable of becoming good." And not only good or even better, but absolutely the best, since the end of it all is transforming communion with God in himself.

Providence can be said to convert evil into good in three general ways. The first is after the manner of Job. A defeat diverts our energies towards more propitious endeavors, but on the same level of human means and ends: for example, the merchant who loses his/her whole business in a fire. This misfortune forces him/her to start the same business all over again, but this time s/he becomes even more prosperous than before.

The second way occurs when a fall, a setback or a failure diverts our energies toward more spiritual pursuits. These are the many *felix culpas* which dot our existence: the knife which prunes, the sin which brings us to our senses, the accident which changes the whole course of our life. This is evident in the lives of many people. They are thereby forced to a deeper level of activity and receptivity.

In each of the first two modes, providence allows us to see some concrete results from our suffering. We can say that at least eventually we come to understand something of why our defeat had to happen in the first place, or why it had to occur in a particular manner. Our minds and hearts are at least partially at rest, for now we see a reason. We are somewhat satisfied. It was a blessing in disguise, a happy chance.

But what about the far more common and much more difficult situations in which our understanding remains completely frustrated and totally in the dark—the situations where we cannot see any good coming out of evil? What about those frequent instances where no profit can be perceived on any material or spiritual level to counterbalance the diminishment? For instance, a crib death, an irreconcilable divorce, ravaging famines, suppression of human rights by brute force, genocide. These pertain to the third way in which providence transfers evil into good. In fact, "this is the most efficacious and the most sanctifying of all ways."

C. Communion with God in Faith through Diminishment

In what concerns the mystery of faith—especially the darkness of faith—Teilhard's convictions accord profoundly with those of St. John of the Cross. Both men imbibe deeply from the Gospel and from Christian tradition. Teilhard's insights on the obscurity of faith in relation to diminishments—particularly on the epitome of all diminishments, death—are especially noteworthy.

First of all, what does he mean by the expression, "the darkness of faith"? "I, as much as anyone, walk in the darkness *[les ombres]* of faith. . . . In order to account for this darkness, which is so contradictory to divine light, some spiritual masters try to explain that the Lord intentionally hides himself from us to test our love. One would have to be irretrievably lost in mental gymnastics or completely insensitive to the agonizing doubts within oneself and in others not to perceive the inveterate inhumanness of such a solution. . . . To my mind, this darkness *[obscurité]* of faith is simply a particular instance of the problem of evil. . . . If God allows us to suffer, to sin and to doubt, it is because he cannot immediately and in one fell swoop heal us and manifest himself completely to us. And if he cannot, it is solely because we are still incapable of letting him do it, since we have not yet passed beyond our pilgrim state."[6]

Concerning the mystery of death, Teilhard considers every diminishment a kind of death. Death, properly speaking, is the definitive detachment of the human person from every experiential point of reference *(tout cadre expérimental);* that is, from every framework that is perceptible or tangible in this life. Each detachment is a particular severance from some point of reference in our mortal world. All our daily deaths are recapitulated and consummated in the end by our personal death. Thus, for each of us living in faith (Gal. 2:20), death becomes the only way truly capable of definitively detaching us and wrenching us from all that is not God in himself.

But, in order that faith be unconditional surrender to ineffable love, complete darkness in relation to every experimental framework is necessary. Otherwise, we will not let go. We will irresistibly hang on for dear life.

Therefore, only our loving Father, who knows exactly what we need in its proper measure, can prune us in such a way as to preserve in us all that is transformable in himself, while cutting away all that is not capable of becoming divinized (John 15:1–5).

Teilhard expresses the intensity and all-embraciveness of our abandonment in darkest faith to God through the symbol of the *orans,* or perhaps more precisely of the *adorans.* "To adore. That means to become lost in the Unfathomable, to plunge into the Inexhaustible, to find peace in the Incorruptible. . . . It is to offer oneself to the" all-consuming and transforming "Fire of divine love, to let oneself consciously and voluntarily be annihilated in the measure that one becomes aware" of one's inner poverty. "To adore means to give of one's deepest to him whose depth has no end." In sum, "to adore is to lose oneself unitively in God."[7]

Yet, why can unreserved surrender to God in faith be accomplished only in total darkness? Teilhard's explanation parallels closely that of the Mystical Doctor.

A first response stems from the overpowering nature of faith as divine light. This light, which of itself is so pure and illuminating, has an obscuring effect on our powers of comprehension and understanding. This is so because we are still incapable of going beyond the limitations of this life. Only the complete detachment wrought by death can definitively break through these limitations.

Another response arises from the paradoxically positive role that darkness plays in the intensification of abandonment in faith. Darkness does not cause faith, nor an increase in faith. God alone is its cause (together with our voluntary cooperation). However, darkness is the necessary condition for an increase in faith. The more we walk in darkness, the more we are providentially disposed for true surrender. When darkness is total, abandonment to the Other is perfect. That is, in essence, what death so effectively accomplishes. It is precisely the situation of complete darkness in death which allows us to pass into total Light.

All that is of life in our being spontaneously abhors darkness and letting go. We instinctively reach out for some support, some crutch. If allowed to have its way, this aspect of our humanness would effectively impede our adoration. It is necessary, therefore, that every suppport be taken from us, ultimately even that of our earthly existence. This is exactly what the darkness element of faith accomplishes. It eliminates progressively all the supports we try to cling to. It ultimately removes even the possibility of clinging to anything. Darkness forms the concrete milieu in which we have no one and nothing else to depend on except God himself.

At the outset of our journey in faith, God leaves much of the initiative for our purification to us. Through self-knowledge we perceive certain attachments in our life. We then take calculated measures to remove these obstacles in order to continue our passage through creation. We detach ourselves to the degree that we can. Gradually, however, as we perceive the limitations of our efforts and the preponderant efficacy of God's activity within us, this initiative is tranformed into abandonment to him. God uses all these passivities of existence to actualize our potential. Yet, of all these passivities, those of diminishment are the most sanctifying, since they are also the most detaching. In their darkness they favor most efficaciously the full development of surrender in faith.

In this way, God does not directly darken the soul, and he certainly takes no pleasure in pain or death. Rather, he unites us to himself and divinizes us, but in a manner which respects completely the laws of our mortal being. God permits the normal activity of the interior and exterior forces of growth and of diminishment to ascend towards definitive metamorphosis. These diminishments in themselves represent the destruction of being. Yet, through these same diminishments and beyond the darkness which they cause, God is encountered in faith and love.

Communion with God through death coincides then with his victory (and ours in him) over evil. Nonetheless, true victory over evil is situated in the realm of faith, beyond evil itself. Evil as such is not directly destroyed. It does not have to be. For, left to itself, as we transcend it by faith, evil self-destructs, falling back by its own weight into the multiple (i.e., into what the Gospel calls exterior darkness). This occurs in and through the personal death of each individual. It will happen collectively at the end of the world.

The dying Christ conquered evil not by destroying it directly, but rather by not letting it destroy him, even though it literally killed him. Jesus allowed evil to destroy itself in trying to destroy him. (Deicide is the absolute epitome of all conceivable and actual evil.) In his death, Christ passed through evil to the Father. In death, by his interior act of total submission to the Father as well as by his theandric love for him and for creation, Jesus allowed his divinity to permeate completely his humanity, thereby transforming it in God and detaching it from all the limitations of this mortal existence. Yes, Christ surely resisted evil right up to the point of death in that he did not allow it to vanquish him interiorly. Jesus's submission was to the Father alone. He never capitulated to evil. So too for us in him. By abandonment in faith, we rise with Christ above and beyond every death, leaving evil behind in outer darkness.

Thus, the true Christian prays, "It is not enough, Lord, to die while communing with you. Teach me to commune in the act of dying itself." Not only does communion with God eventually and literally cause each person to pass from this life, but also we experience in faith real communion with God through the darkness of the very act of dying.

D. True Christian Resignation

For Teilhard, our attitude towards diminishments comprises two essential elements: maximum effort against whatever is of evil in them, and maximum receptivity towards God alone through them and beyond them. This is active submission to the Father's will, whether we are speaking of the obedience of Jesus to the Father or of our obedience to him in Christ. Resignation is truly Christian only inasmuch as we make a vigorous resistance with God against evil. This resistance arises from our unlimited abandonment to and trust in him beyond evil.

If we do not do everything within our power to resist a given evil, we do not find ourselves with the particular quality of receptivity willed by God. Consequently, we cannot undergo him as much as we could have otherwise. If our effort is courageous and persevering, we rejoin God through the evil, beyond the evil. In this way, "the optimum of our communion in resignation" indeed "coincides with the maximum of our fidelity to human endeavor."

However, we must not conceive of this effort against evil and this receptivity to God as successive elements, the one follow-

101

ing the other. Both coexist concomitantly from the beginning and endure right up to the end. On the one hand, this maximum effort safeguards our receptivity so that it does not become capitulation to evil rather than submission to God beyond evil. On the other hand, our abandonment to God from the beginning ensures that the effort in question is not against God, but is uniquely against evil. Christian resignation is not just something residual, as if it were merely a consequence of all else having failed. Christian resignation is inherently positive, because it is toward God. In this manner, the faithful person is not, properly speaking, resigned either to suffering or to death. We are resigned only to God, deeper than the pain and beyond the death. The faith-filled person must resist all suffering and death with every ounce of his/her strength. And when exterior resistance becomes no longer possible, like that of Christ our interior resistance must continue right up to the very end. The final human act of each one of us in faith is always toward Life beyond death.

True Christian resignation emerges, then, as the point of convergence between the struggle against evil and our receptivity to God alone. It is the point where God exercises his full primacy over us as we abandon ourselves totally to him.

Having resisted evil for God with all our force, we arrive sooner or later at inevitable defeat (defeat, that is, according to our experimental framework). This is the hour par excellence of Christian resignation. For if we accept this diminishment "in faith, without ceasing to struggle against diminishment, the diminishment itself can become for us a loving source of renewal. . . . In the realm of faith a further dimension exists which allows God to effect imperceptibly a mysterious reversal of evil into good. Leaving behind the zone of human successes and failures, the Christian reaches by an effort of trust in the One greater than him/herself the region of supersensible transformations and growths. This resignation is but a movement that transposes the field of his/her activity into a higher realm."

Thus, death is not only *le Mal*, but it coincides especially and in a transcendent manner with the recapitulation and consummation of all Christian resignation. Death is the apex of communion with God in darkest faith. It is the loss of self in One greater than self. Death becomes the place of limitless abandonment to God in himself.

Notes from Chapter 4

1. All quotations unless otherwise identified in this chapter are found in *DM*, pp. 74–94.

2. *Writings*, p. 261. See *Contemplation*, pp. 117–122.

3. *Writings*, p. 260.

4. *Cor.*, p. 31; *HE*, p. 38.

5. *Night*, I, 14, 4. See *Contemplation*, pp. 85–96.

6. *CE*, pp. 131–132. Whether or not Teilhard includes John of the Cross among those spiritual masters *(docteurs)* is conjectural. In any case what Teilhard justifiably criticizes does not represent the Sanjuanist position.

7. *DM*, pp. 127–128; *TF*, p. 65.

Chapter 5

Receptivity of a Superior Order

In *The Mystical Milieu* (1917), Teilhard refers to a certain receptivity of a superior order. "In his/her eagerness to undergo the domination of God, there was a time when the mystic found him/herself forced into action. Now, however, the process is reversed. The very excess of his/her desire for action orientates him/her towards *une passivité d'ordre supérieur*."[1]

At the end of the same essay, Teilhard goes on to insist that what he had written was only an introduction to mysticism and that he does not believe that he possesses the necessary qualifications to describe the sublime states of transforming union.

Is he too modest, or is he confessing a real incompetency? Neither. At the age of thirty-six, Teilhard was not yet sufficiently qualified to analyze in depth the advanced stages of this mysticism, even though he discerned their existence and situated them quite well in the overall development of interior progress. Later in life, however, he does take up some of the elements which constitute true mystical union. Needless to say, he expresses these elements in his own inimitable way.

Before we take up these expressions, let us examine more closely what Teilhard means in general by the phrase "receptivity of a superior order."

When referring to the passivities of existence, of growth or of diminishment, Teilhard consistently employs the plural, *les passivités*. In the context of a superior order, however, the word *passivité* is used in the singular. This is so because, in the context of a superior order, he is not referring directly to a host of influences. Instead, he is stressing a basic interior attitude, that of remaining receptive before a variety of situations which converge on God's influence within us. It is a question of our fundamental stance towards all passivities. This attitude of receptivity increases in proportion to our christification as God brings us into the advanced states of transforming union. At these thresholds—which St. John of the Cross calls night of spirit, tranquil night, serene night, spiritual espousals, spiritual marriage[2]—our receptivity is permeated by an intensity and a quality which are truly of a superior order. It is indeed "superior" in comparison to whatever we had previously experienced.

In the concluding paragraphs of *The Mystical Milieu*,[3] Teilhard reveals some of his insights concerning the superior quality of this receptivity:

"Already at the earliest dawning of the mystical movement within the soul, God is experienced as the only One who can sustain it and direct it." Authentic mystical experience is received entirely from God. Moreover, it is completely sustained and directed by him alone.

"The zest for life *[le goût de vivre]* which is the source of all our passion and of all our wisdom does not arise from ourselves. . . . It is God himself who must give us even the impulse to seek him." Yes, we undergo life as much as, if not more than, we undergo death. Not only is our individual act of existence received, but also all our potentiality for becoming greater. Moreover, not only the potentiality to become, but also its very actualization is received. "We cannot do other than receive ourselves *[nous ne faisons que nous recevoir]*."

"And even though the soul experiences itself on fire for heaven, it still cannot by itself see what it lacks in order to get there." This expresses the quintessence of passive purifications; namely, even with the assistance of the most competent spiritual direction, we come to know ourselves only up to a certain point. Beyond that point, God alone has the power to penetrate our innermost being so as to detach us from every trace of egocentrism. We let it be done by him.

"And when, finally, the soul has discerned the flaming Center that has been seeking it out, it remains powerless of itself to follow the divine Light all the way. . . . For it is written: 'No one comes to me unless I take him and myself draw him into me' "(John 6:44). Teilhard concludes: "The beatitude of mystical union is consummated in the realization of the absolutely gratuitous act of this supreme dependence on God."

Thus, we understand the simple meaning of *passivité d'ordre supérieur:* Everything which is done in us in order to divinize us is done by God.

Throughout the course of his life, Teilhard affords various concrete examples and specific insights regarding this receptivity of a superior order. Among these we select the most important and group them under the following five headings: (1) the meaning of the Cross; (2) the spiritual power of Matter; (3) Teilhard's third way; (4) detachment by passing all the way through and by sublimation; (5) the saying, "Everything that happens is adorable." Under some of these headings we shall treat the subject in a more or less systematic fashion. In several instances, however, we shall apply this receptive attitude in a concrete manner to the situation at hand.

1. The Meaning of the Cross

By its very nature the Cross has always been a principle of selection and a sign of contradiction. The Cross inherently makes no sense at all (1 Cor. 1:18, 22–24). Yet, in faith it becomes "a sublime goal that we attain in transcending ourselves." The Cross is "the symbol, the way and the act itself of making Progress."[4]

Teilhard calls the Cross the symbol of Progress because it is the Christian sign par excellence of Christ carrying the weight of a World in Progress. Jesus on the Cross symbolizes the blood, sweat and tears of all generations trying to make something better out of their lives and out of their world for themselves, for their progeny and for God. It is the way—indeed the only way (John 14:6)—because true spiritualization is accomplished solely through detachment from every experimental point of reference. "Our daily deaths together with our personal death are but so many thresholds sown along the road to Union."[5] The Cross is the very act of Progress by reason of the principle that Teilhard reiterated in so many different ways. "The more perfect the Union, the more intense must be the suffering."[6] Or, as he expressed it in *The Phenomenon of Man* (1940, pp. 50—51): "Every synthesis costs something. . . . Nothing worthwhile is ever made except at the price of an equivalent destruction of energy. . . . As a matter of fact, from the real evolutionary standpoint, something is necessarily burnt up in the course of every synthesis in order to pay for it."

Thus, the Cross is a sublime goal, but not in the sense of an end in itself. God is our sole End. The Cross is a goal in the sense of a necessary condition in order to attain transforming union in him.

In its most general sense, the reality of the Cross effects the basic separation among men and women. It distinguishes the courageous from the pleasure-seekers. It separates the serious from the frivolous, the sincere from the takers, men from mice. Whether one uses the word "cross," "night," "self-discipline," "asceticism," "mysticism," or any other term, the effect is the same: Each person convinced that true Progress lies up ahead at the cost of intense personal effort and suffering adheres by this very fact to the doctrine of the Cross. Life has but one term, and it imposes only one direction: "Towards the highest possible spiritualization by means of maximum effort." Whoever makes his/her best effort to improve the World has already begun in his/her own way to follow the crucified Jesus, since all conscientious human activity is necessarily an ascesis.[7]

To this general, human disposition Christianity offers certain specific insights. First, the mystery of "the sin of the world" (John 1:29) provides the deepened perception of the moral and physical weaknesses inherent in the evolutionary process. Second, the unfathomable reality of the historical Jesus, especially in his passion and death, reveals without doubt that true growth and goodness "is not to be sought in the temporal zones of our visible world, but that the effect required of our fidelity must be consummated beyond a total metamorphosis of ourselves and of everything around us."

The Cross means "detachment from the sensate World, and even in a certain sense, rupture with this World." The Cross is the way of "a veritable positive 'annihilation' which is born of the very paroxysm of our development."[8] "It is the road of human effort supernaturally rectified and extended."

From a hedonistic point of view, suffering and death (even effort and discipline) constitute the slagheap of nature and particularly of humanity. It is so much waste, futility, rubbish to be done away with, buried or incinerated. But to the person of prayer and faith, the Cross recycles, so to speak, all this debris in the direction of Spirit.

From a purely pragmatic standpoint, long-term and terminal sufferers should be put out of their misery. They are useless drains on society's resources. For whatever reason, they are failures and must not be allowed to obstruct progress. The mystery of the Cross manifests not only the inhumanness of such attitudes, but also the fact that they are absolutely unchristian. For, from the perspective of the Body of Christ, there are many different organs and diverse functions. That charism which is most charged with

108

potential to advance the spiritual Progress of the World is the *adorans*, the contemplative. By circumstance and by providence, sufferers are forced out of the realm of exterior and material development into the realm of interior and spiritual Progress—a veritable contemplative life. Thus, in a most intense manner, sufferers carry the weight of our World in Progress. By a mysterious act of providence, they have paradoxically the capacity to become the most active contributors to the same development that seems to have victimized them.[9]

If the image of the Cross is the sublime goal and the way of spiritual transformation, then Jesus upon his Cross is both the symbol and the reality of the immense labor necessary in order to liberate spirit. The crucified Christ represents and recapitulates all the effort of creation struggling together with God "to ascend the slopes of being, at times holding on to creatures to find support, at other times being detached from them in order to go beyond them. . . . The Cross, consequently, is not something inhuman, but something vastly superhuman. . . . For the Christian, it is not a question of swooning in its shadow, but of ascending in the light of the Cross."

Yes, the Cross is definitely not something inhuman, but superhuman. The receptivity which allows us to accept joyously this truth is indeed *une passivité d'ordre supérieur*.

2. The Spiritual Power of Matter

"Matter is the ensemble of things, energies, creatures which surround us. . . . It is the common, universal, tangible milieu infinitely varied and shifting within which we live."[10]

Matter thus defined presents itself to us to be acted upon in two ways. On the one hand, it is a burden. It fetters. It is the prime source of pain and sin which threaten our lives. It weights us down. It wounds us and tempts us. Matter makes us grow old, paralyzed, vulnerable, guilty. Who will deliver us from this body doomed to death? (Rom. 7:24).

Yet, on the other hand and at the same time, Matter is what nourishes and uplifts us. "It is physical exuberance, ennobling contact, virile effort, the joy of growth. Matter attracts, renews, unites, flowers. By Matter we are linked to everything else." Who will give us an immortal body? (1 Cor. 15:42–53).

Matter is a fundamental principle of both death and life.

In order to illustrate the paradoxes of Matter, Teilhard makes use of two comparisons: (1) that of the diver who wants to surface from the depths of the sea, and (2) that of the mountain climber who, facing a slope enveloped in fog, struggles to climb to the summit bathed in light. These two images have three points in common with our inner selves in regard to Matter. First, space is divided into two zones with opposing characteristics; the one behind appears ever darker, while the one up ahead becomes progressively more luminous. Second, we are the ones who ascend or descend. Matter provides the support necessary for our movement. Third, in the course of our effort, the light ahead increases with each forward advance, while the darkness behind increases.

In itself, therefore, and prior to any position or choice on our part, Matter is simply the slope on which we can just as easily go up or go down. "By nature and as a result of the sin of the world, matter represents. . . a perpetual tendency towards entropy. But, also by nature and as a consequence of the incarnation, it offers us the spur and the allurement to be our accomplice towards heightened being. This counterbalances and eventually dominates the former tendency." Each of us finds ourselves situated, then, at a particular point somewhere on the slope. In order to advance towards light, certain creatures are placed in our path not as obstacles, but as footholds to pass beyond and as intermediaries to be made use of. The concrete possibilities are as numerous as the charisms proper to each individual. There is a St. Peter and a St. Paul as well as a John of the Cross and a Teilhard de Chardin.

110

Upon the slope, true separation is made not exactly between Matter and Spirit, but rather between carnal and spiritual. As a result of our initial position on the slope and as a result of each position which we thereafter occupy on it, Matter is divided according to our effort and our intention into two zones: "Matter in the material and carnal sense" (that which tends towards entropy), and "Matter in a spiritual sense" (that which we make use of in our spiritualization). Over the long haul, two gifts gradually dominate our movement towards the summit: contemplation and chastity. The first represents what is deepest in the mystical thrust. The second sums up the ascetical effort.[11]

All this describes the general ascent of Matter toward Spirit. In virtue of Christ's incarnation, death and resurrection, all evolution is being directed toward the Parousia. It is in Christogenesis. The movement is one: toward the highest possible degree of being. Its rhythm is twofold: immersion and emergence.

"Matter, in you I find both seduction and strength, caresses and virility. You can enrich me or destroy me. I surrender myself to your mighty layers trusting in the heavenly influences which have penetrated and purified your deep waters. The power of Christ has passed into you. May your allurement draw me forward. May your sap nourish me. May your resistance make me strong. May your detachments free me. And, finally may your whole being become the matrix of my divinization."

The abandonment of oneself to Matter with such deep conviction and determination is extraordinary in the history of spirituality. In order not to succumb to the temptation of matter, Teilhard would surely be in need of a special grace, a grace emanating from a receptivity of a superior order. In fact he expressed just such an awareness in his *Journal* (April 23, 1919): "My life must be a great example of obedience—passively accomplished—to the universal operation of God: a great act of faith in the 'spiritual power of Matter.' "

Toward the end of his life, in *The Heart of Matter* (1950, pp. 46–47), Teilhard leaves us a mature reflection concerning the seriousness of this vocation. "Even at my age [sixty-nine], I am still learning by experience just how risky it is for one to be called to leave behind the well-trodden path of a certain traditional asceticism. . . . Yet, I have been forced by grace and by inner necessity to search in the direction of heaven for a way—one not mediocre, but superior—in which all the dynamics of Matter and of Flesh pass into the genesis of Spirit. . . . Yes, to Christify Matter! That sums up the whole venture of my interior life. Although I am still often frightened by this pursuit, I have never been able to do other than take the required risk."

3. Teilhard's Third Way

Just what is this way that is not mediocre, but superior?

In a certain sense, Teilhard's *via tertia* synthesizes his spirituality. It also sheds considerable light on the meaning he gives to the word "superior" in the phrase "receptivity of a superior order."

In effect, Teilhard's third way is a succinct formulation of a complex and all-embracive reality. He uses it often in the sense of a *via media;* that is, a way between two extremes, a way out of a dilemma, a way through an impasse. This middle or third way, however, is far from compromising, mediocre or neutral. "It is a superior and daring way which recapitulates and corrects the values and characteristics of the other two ways," whatever they may be in a specific situation.[12] This third way is like a synthesis in a dialectic, like a threshold in an evolution, like an emergence in a genesis.

In other words, the mysticism of the *via tertia* can take two opposing factions, digest out of them what is really of Spirit in each, and synthesize this into something superior to either or both. In Teilhard's personal life, the question underlying this *via media* was experienced in an acute form of dualism: either love of Heaven or love of the Earth; either cult of Spirit or cult of Matter. It took him almost half his life to resolve the dilemma for himself: "We must go to Heaven through the Earth. There exists true communion with God through the World. Moreover, to give oneself completely to this truth is not to contradict the Gospel and to try to serve two masters [Matt. 6:24]. . . . No, between the cult of Spirit which requires us to flee Matter and the cult of Matter which forces us to deny Spirit" there is another possibility: namely, "detachment no longer by running away from, but by passing all the way through and by sublimation. Spiritualization is not accomplished by negation of or withdrawal from creatures, but by" convergence with them in Christ and "emergence beyond them in him."[13]

Perhaps nowhere is this truth applied in a more down-to-earth fashion than in the question of celibate love. Teilhard experienced the agony and the ecstasy of this gift as keenly as anyone. In fact, he perceived the ability to love both deeply and celibately at the same time as the ultimate test of his theology of attaining Spirit through Matter. "The living heart of the Tangible is the Flesh," he wrote in 1950, "and for Man, Flesh is Woman. . . . At the term of the spiritual power of Matter lies the spiritual power of the Flesh and of the Feminine."[14]

Teilhard certainly does not intend the above expressions to be taken in any kind of chauvinistic manner. Nor are they pro-feminist, anti-feminist or sexist in any way. On the contrary, he is trying desperately to return to the pristine message of the Gospel and to learn from the incarnation and the resurrection how to grow in/through/with his deep love for a particular woman and his love for Christ in the context of a celibate vocation. He experienced each of these loves as special graces, not to be lived like parallel lines, but as divine gifts converging one upon the other in a deeper synthesis. Moreover, he was convinced that until he could integrate his love in interior peace and joy despite whatever surface turbulence and tension might persist, his convictions about the spiritual power of Matter would remain only a pipe dream.

"Theoretically this transformation of love is quite possible.

All that is needed to effect it is that the pull of the personal divine Center (Christ) be experienced with sufficient force to transform our natural attraction. . . .

"In practice, I must admit the difficulty of such an undertaking. . . . Surely, you say, universal experience has proven conclusively that spiritual loves have always ended up in the mud. Well, you said also that man is meant to walk with his feet firmly on the ground. Who could have ever dreamt that he would fly? [Much less walk on the moon!]

"Yes, I respond, some dreamers have dared. . . . Yet, what paralyzes Life is the lack of faith and the refusal to risk. Life's greatest difficulty does not lie in solving problems [or in answering questions], but rather in posing them correctly. . . .

"Thus, the day will surely come"—indeed it is already here!—"when, after harnessing space, gravity, the winds and the tides, we shall harness for God the energies of love. And on that day, for the second time in the history of the World, man will have discovered fire."[15]

Needless to say, the grace to live day-in and day-out all the formidable exigencies of this *via tertia* does not pertain to any passivity of a compromising, mediocre or half way. It can arise only out of a courageous receptivity to and of a superior order.

4. Detachment by Passing All the Way through and by Sublimation

Throughout this book the question of detachment has recurred in a variety of contexts and from diverse points of view. Here we propose a synthesis of Teilhard's teaching on the subject, stressing some of his particular insights.

From an evolutionary perspective, detachment can no longer be primarily understood as a rupture with the World (although something in that view is valid), but rather as ɔ passing all the way through creation and as a sublimation of it: *détachement par traversée et sublimation*. Let us examine each truth contained in the above affirmation in order to appreciate better Teilhard's unique contributions.

A. Detachment Viewed from an Evolutionary Perspective

In *The Phenomenon of Man* (1940, p. 218), Teilhard expresses not only his personal theories and Christian extrapolations regarding evolution, but also responds emphatically to a frequently asked question: "Is evolution a theory, a system or a hypothesis? It is much more. It is a general condition to which all theories, all hypotheses, all systems must bow and which they must henceforth satisfy if they are to be thinkable and true. Evolution is a light illuminating all facts; a curve that all lines must follow." Even ascetical-mystical theology! There exist innumerable theories and hypotheses regarding the particulars of the evolutionary process (even more today than in Teilhard's time). But development, evolution and genesis as a general condition is an indisputable fact. It has always been integral to the process by which God effects transforming union.

Thus, long before Darwin or Teilhard, true Christian mystics have been caught up and swept along by a dynamic élan emanating from deep within the Gospel. This élan ascends relentlessly toward the Parousia. It has always been at the very soul of Christian mysticism. From the beginning, the person of Jesus has constituted its Alpha, its Way and its Omega (Rev. 22:13; John 14:6). Yet, the scientific discovery of evolution as an all-embracive reality has shed enormous light on the mystery of life, especially interior life. Even though scientific evolution as such has been preoccupied almost exclusively with the outside of things *(le dehors)*, it remains Teilhard's outstanding personal contribution to have uncovered scientifically the within of things *(le dedans)*.

115

So, how does this affect the high school dropout or the illiterate peasant? What does this mean to the humble mendicant of centuries past or to the otherwise sincere person of today who still is skeptical about scientific evolution?

Teilhard responds, "One can be extremely 'cosmic' in affection and in tendency, while at the same time remaining rigorously detached in the narrowest and most austere sense of the term. That is, a Trappist can actually live a truly open interior life, even if he still thinks that the world is flat and that he must be cut off from all its machinations. . . . Stark detachment, such as that practiced by the great contemplative orders, should not be viewed in contrast to or in rupture with the arduous labor of cosmic Evolution. On the contrary, their asceticism is a flourishing and a prolongation of the latter," even if they do not directly advert to the fact.[16]

"It would not only be useless, but also wrong to try to find in the Saints of the past explicit approval or condemnation of what I call cosmic asceticism, since the question of Evolution proper never entered their minds. What we do need to be able to perceive, however, is that, when we translate their quest for holiness into today's terms, we are able to see that indeed their detachment was by beyond-attachment *[détachement par surat-tachement]*." That is, that their ascesis of spiritualization was not in effect "anti-Matter or extra-Matter, but trans-Matter."[17]

B. Detachment No Longer Understood Primarily as a Rupture with the World

By reason of the element of discontinuity inherent in the evolutionary process, there is quite literally a leaving behind, a separation, a kind of rupture in every detachment. This is most evident in the case of death. Furthermore, whatever pertains to the machinations, to the self-centeredness, to the self-indulgent

116

elements of the world (John 1:10–11) quite obviously must be cut off and left to fall away (John 15:1–5; Matt. 13:43, 50).

Teilhard's point in this regard, however, is that the negative element is not primary. It flows only as a consequence from the primary positive thrust. It is because conversion is towards God that we turn away from sin. It is because our commitment is to Christ that we consequently give up whatever is holding us back from further christification.

During Teilhard's time the following phrase often recurred in the prayers of the Mass and the Breviary: *Da nobis, Domine, terrena despicere* (Grant us, Oh Lord, to despise everything terrestrial). Needless to say, that phrase used to irritate Teilhard no end. Nonetheless, he did try to give it as favorable an interpretation as possible: "Fortunately, this sentiment can be reconciled with 'cosmic love' if we understand *despicere* in the sense of 'to regard as secondary' and *terrena* as 'things loved for themselves without reference to Christ.' Nevertheless, it seems that there has been an important evolution in Christian thought on this subject. Sanctification is envisaged less as a work of rupture with or withdrawal from creation than as a love of detached involvement *[un amour du travail désintéressé]*."[18]

What is this detached involvement, or, as he expressed it in *The Divine Milieu* (1927, p. 120), a passionate equilibrium regarding all things *(une indifférence passionée)*?

C. Detachment by Passing All the Way through Creation and by Sublimation

Teilhard has his own way of expressing the dialectic of *todo* and *nada: tout m'est Tout, et tout ne m'est rien; tout m'est Dieu, et tout m'est poussière.*[19] That is, everything is both All to me and nothing; it is both God to me and dust. Every creature is from God, to God and, with the proper distinctions, is capable of being transformed in God. But it is still not God, nor will it ever become God in himself.

The above truth constitutes the gist of what Teilhard calls cosmic life, cosmic love, cosmic ascesis, cosmic mysticism. The ability to live this truth peacefully and joyfully is what constitutes a fully integrated Christian.

Teilhard's theology of suffering and mortification sheds considerable light on the above terminology. Most eighteenth- and nineteenth-century interpretations of suffering can be summarized thus: Suffering is first and foremost a punishment, an expiation. Its effectiveness derives from the fact that it hurts. In fact, the more it hurts, the better it is. It is born of sin and makes up for sin. It is good to suffer, to deny oneself, to inflict pain and deprivation upon oneself. This is sacrifice, penance, reparation.

In contrast to that view, an evolutionary perspective sheds a very different light. Suffering and detachment are primarily the consequence of the labor of development and the price that has to be paid for it. Their effectiveness derives from the generosity of the effort, the blood, sweat, tears involved in trying to make a better World for Christ. Physical and moral evil are the by-products of the process of becoming, for everything that develops suffers and commits its own faults. The Cross is the symbol of the arduous task of Evolution. This is how the sin of the World is taken away. This may be called evangelical poverty, Christian asceticism, *détachement par traversée*.

Detachment by going all the way through denotes this: In full discipleship with the Incarnate Word, we become deeply involved not only with creation as the sum total of creatures, but also with creation as the ongoing process of Evolution. We become involved all the way through to its very term—recapitulation of all in Christ (Col. 1:20). If we become so involved with him in his involvement, then we must go all the way and die with him in all so as to rise with him beyond all.

At this point, Teilhard adds a further insight: sublimation.

Detachment not only *par traversée,* but also *par sublimation.*

In true detached involvement there exist not only discontinuity with respect to creatures, but also continuity. Passing through creation, we bring along with us in a purified and transformed manner the quintessence of everything in our World. In this sense, detachment is not exactly the opposite of attachment, In other words, it is "a kind of transformed attachment like spirit is transformed matter and internationalism is transformed patriotism."[20] In this way, we abandon ourselves to creatures with passionate equilibrium. We experience in their regard—with equal truth—that we have need of everything and that we have need of nothing. The One-Thing-Necessary comprises everything.

On the occasion of his interior crisis-conversion during the battle of Verdun, Teilhard expresses in his *Journal* (July 17, 1916) a very personal and insightful integration of all these elements. "We must go to God with all our heart [Matt. 22:37]. This means not only our heart as a capacity for loving, but especially our heart as actually filled with concrete loves. . . . Our conversion to God does not consist in emptying our heart and substituting him for all our loves. No, our conversion rather consists in assimilating in him all our loves in their concrete fullness," letting God purify them and transform them. This is a truly integrated Christian life.

Thus, God is encountered in those we love to the degree that both we and they become more and more spiritualized. Christ is not a substitution for our loves. Rather, these loves must be sublimated in him. They must become integrated in his love. Attachment and detachment—like breathing in and breathing out. That is the true breath of the mystic.

Could anyone seriously doubt that this lived experience in all its day-in and day-out implications must pertain to a receptivity of a superior order?

Yes, you say, that's great for an active person, an active spirituality. But what about the contemplative? Isn't contemplative life one of all renunciation with no involvement? Detachment by withdrawal? Oh, you of little faith! (Not to mention of little understanding!) The true mystic, the real contemplative, is the person most involved in the World, and therefore necessarily also the most detached. For s/he has gone all the way through to the very Heart of Matter, to the very Core of the Universe—there where the Action and Passion really are—sublimating all in All.

5. "Everything that Happens Is Adorable"

Tout ce qui arrive est adorable. "Properly understood," Teilhard adds, "that saying summarizes the core of my religious conviction."[21] It also explains in a very practical way the continual and eventually final dominance of renunciation in God over personal progress. Put another way, ultimate personal progress is achieved only in total surrender of self to God.

Teilhard had used a variation of this saying when he first spoke of the passivities of existence. "Oh, 'the joy of the action of the Other within us!' That is exactly what makes the passivities of existence appear so delicate to me and so worthy of adoration."[22] Moreover, Teilhard charges the French *adorable* with much more force than its English equivalent normally conveys. "To adore means to give of one's deepest to him whose depth has no end. . . . to lose oneself unitively in God."[23]

Gradually, as he became more imbued with a receptivity of a superior order, Teilhard reflected ever more deeply on the significance of all passivities precisely as *adorables*. In his *Retreat Notes* of October 21–29, 1944, he gives that phrase its necessary nuances. In effect he affirms that whatever befalls us, whether good or bad, eventually becomes adorable on the condition that we have done everything within our power "to give Christic energy its full meaning and its full being in the Universe."[24] In other words, on condition that we have done our maximum to bestow on creatures the utmost reality that Christ desires us to give them, and also on condition that we have left ourselves receptive to imbibe the maximum spiritual energy with which they have to endow us, only then in his providence is anything truly *adorable*.

Furthermore, the word *adorable* is not only an adjective. It also has the force of a noun, a proper name: *l'Adorable*. For "Whatever we suffer, we suffer Christ." That is, we undergo Christ himself while he suffers in us, with us. He and I suffer each other together. We suffer each other for one another and on account of each other. *"Com-patimur."*[25]

This is the ultimate in true Christian resignation. This is to commune with God in the deepest way possible this side of the resurrection. To experience *l'Adorable* in everything that happens is unquestionably a receptivity of a superior order.

6. Summary

Some spiritual authors have tried to summarize ascetical-mystical theology in vast syntheses. We think of Rodriguez, Tanquerey, Garrigou-Lagrange and more recently Royo-Aumann. These are almost like textbooks. They offer a relative service, but they lack the personal touch of the lived experience.

Neither St. John of the Cross nor Teilhard attempted a compendium of spirituality. Each described his own communion with God in his way and according to his particular gift. Their words, their sentences, their paragraphs flowed out of a deep, moving faith, and they simply let the pieces fall where they might. Neither was concerned about being published: John, because the possibility never really entered his mind; Teilhard, because the immediate possiblity was removed by ecclesiastical edict. They were not even concerned with polishing their writings, getting imprimaturs or satisfying this critic or that. John and Teilhard were simply themselves, and they let their written expression reflect their uniqueness in Christ Jesus.

In this vein, therefore, let us summarize all that we have been considering regarding the mystery of receptivity in Teilhard with a very homespun confession of his written in 1924. "Spiritual authors dispute whether activity should precede contemplation as a preparation for it, or whether it should flow from contemplation as a divine superabundance of it. I must confess that such pseudo-problems mean absolutely nothing to me. Whether I am active or whether I am praying, whether I laboriously open my soul to God through work or whether he assails my soul with passivities from within or from without, I am equally conscious in all instances of being united to/in Christ Jesus. . . . First, foremost and always I am in *Christo Jesu*, and only afterwards do I act, or do I suffer or do I contemplate."[26]

That is the caliber of receptivity proclaimed and lived in the Gospel.

Notes from Chapter 5

1. *Writings*, p. 144.
2. *Canticle*, 8–40.
3. *Writings*, pp. 148–149.
4. *DM*, pp. 101–104 (and the same for all quotations unless otherwise identified in this section); *FM*, p. 98.
5. *HE*, p. 88.
6. *HE*, p. 87.
7. See *Rom* 1:18–25; 8:18–25; *Writings*, pp. 65–68, 71.
8. Teilhard, letter to Jeanne Mortier, Feb. 15, 1940.
9. See "The Significance and Positive Value of Suffering," (1933), in *HE*, pp. 48–52.
10. *DM* pp. 105–111 (and the same for all quotations unless otherwise identified in this section). See *HM*, pp. 67–77, 225–239.
11. See "The Eternal Feminine" (1918), in *Writings*, pp. 191–202; "The Evolution of Chastity" (1934), in *TF*, pp. 60–87; "The Feminine, or the Unitive" (1950), in *HM*, pp. 58–61.
12. *AE*, p. 56.
13. *AE*, pp. 53–57; *CE*, pp. 76–95.
14. *HM*, p. 58; *TF*, p. 70.

15. "The Evolution of Chastity" (1934), in *TF*, pp. 86–87.
16. *Journal*, Oct. 20 and Nov. 5, 1916.
17. "A Note on the Concept of Christian Perfection," (1942) in *TF*, pp. 105–106.
18. *Journal*, May 10, 1916. See *Cor*., pp. 72–74.
19. *DM*, p. 120; Ibid., pp. 95–101; *Writings*, pp. 70–71, 259–264.
20. *Journal*, May 9, 1921.
21. *LT*, pp. 288–289.
22. *MM*, p. 158.
23. *DM*, pp. 127–128; *TF*, pp. 65.
24. *LT*, p. 294.
25. *Writings*, p. 259; *Journal, Feb. 28, 1919; HM*, p. 204; *DM*, p. 123.
26. *SC*, p. 75.

Phase III

Teilhard de Chardin and
John of the Cross

Preliminary Remarks

In the Introduction to this study of the mystery of receptivity, we posed three questions: (1) According to St. John of the Cross, what is the positive yet purifying role of creatures in our progress toward transforming union? (2) How does Teilhard envisage receptivity vis-à-vis the divine activity within us and all around us? (3) Now, what are the main points of divergence and of convergence between the respective teachings of John and Teilhard? Also, what might be the areas of complementarity and personal contribution of each?

Conclusion

Divergence and Convergence

At the end of his major essay, *The Christic* (March 1955), [1] Teilhard addressed a question which he had often asked himself and which his critics are still posing: namely, how is it that as I look around me I find myself alone? Alone to have seen this immense vision of the World, of the Cosmic Christ, of the Divine Milieu? If I am really the only author in the history of theological reflection to have come up so explicitly with such insights, what objective basis do I have to substantiate my convictions?

Teilhard himself responds with what he calls a threefold evidence:

First, there is the evidence of coherence. Despite certain obvious lacunae, disputable tenets and unanswered questions, the substance of his spirituality is radically in accord with the Gospel. The person of Christ is really at the source of both his theology and his life. Moreover, Teilhard firmly believed that his teachings were grounded on what is most authentic in Christian tradition.

Second, there is the evidence deriving from a certain contagious power of his theology. Although he cannot quote a single author who sees the world exactly the way he does, he nevertheless perceived during his lifetime that countless persons were beginning to sense reality basically as he described it. He was, as it were, merely the spokesman of an idea whose time had finally come. He was articulating a realization that was universally beginning to take root.

Third, there is the evidence of a certain superiority to, yet identity with, what he had been taught. This is the area which pertains more directly to our study of receptivity in Teilhard and John of the Cross. Even though one can readily understand in the context of *The Christic* what Teilhard means by *supériorité* and *identité,* we prefer to use the words complementarity and convergence.

Thus, the question remains: Regarding the mystery of receptivity, is there convergence between Teilhard's spirituality and that of St. John of the Cross? And does Teilhard make a personal and complementary contribution in comparison to the Mystical Doctor?

Numerous factors differentiate John and Teilhard: historical and cultural milieus, particular vocations and personalities, world views and interior experiences. Yet, each experienced a very real coherence with the Gospel as lived in the tradition of the Church. Each experienced the prodigious, contagious power of his insights, even within his own lifetime. And each is recognized for his particular contributions to the mystical élan of Christianity.

Furthermore, each derived much profit from the teachings of previous spiritual masters while remaining remarkably unique and personal in his own perceptions and presentation. In the case of John of the Cross, he imbibed deeply from the Carmelite tradition, notably St. Teresa of Jesus; from the pseudo-Dionysius; from St. Augustine, St. Thomas, the Rheno-Flemish mystics; and from the author of the *Cloud of Unknowing.* As for Teilhard, he received a great deal from St. Augustine, St. Francis of Assisi, the Ignatian tradition, St. Teresa of Jesus, St. John of the Cross, Rodriguez, Lallement, Surin, Newman and St. Therese of the Child Jesus. Nonetheless, with the exception of sacred Scripture, direct references or quotations from any of these past masters by either John or Teilhard are comparatively rare.

Their mystical expression arose out of a profound, intimate experience of God within them; a personal, loving encounter with Father, Son and Spirit. Their respective mysticisms grew out of their unshakeable faith in Christ Jesus and out of their participation in the living tradition of the Church. Their communion in the one God, in the one faith in his Son, and in the one tradition constitutes the fundamental basis of their convergence. That is, John and Teilhard do not converge directly one upon the other, but rather both upon the Other. This truth is also the focal point for authenticating their respective spiritualities.

We might summarize the quintessence of St. John of the Cross's mysticism in these terms: Although he possesses a very intimate and balanced teaching on the immanence of God, he consistently accentuates the divine transcendence and the *nada* of everything created. God's immanence is itself transcendent. John explicitly recognizes the necessity of our involvement in creation and our consequent passing all the way through, but he stresses what lies beyond the passage. To encounter God in himself is infinitely superior to attaining his presence within creation. The quest for God through creatures must lead ultimately to direct and immediate communion with him beyond them all. The Christ of St. John of the Cross is the Jesus of St. Paul and of the Gospel, but John accentuates his kenosis. John's asceticism is founded almost entirely on *desnudez*. Its thrust is positive and dynamic, at the same time straight and narrow. He is the co-reformer of Carmel, the apostle of direct and loving transformation in the Beloved in contemplation.

The quintessence of Teilhard's mysticism can be summarized thus: Although the transcendence of God always remains the beginning and the end of his immanent presence, Teilhard stresses his Diaphany: God all in all (1 Cor. 15:28; Eph. 1:23), God through all. The Christ of Teilhard is the personal Jesus of St. Paul and of the Gospel, but he tends to stress the Cosmic Christ: the Universal Christ, Christ the Evolver. Teilhard's asceticism is also cosmic. It is situated in a renewed World vision. Its transversal movement (going all the way through) is constituted by an immersion into the World for Christ, followed by an emergence through the World with him, with a continual and eventually final dominance of the second over the first. This élan comprises both the vertical and the horizontal in such a way that the *En-Haut* and the *En-Avant* converge towards the Christic. Detachment is accomplished by *surattachement*. Spiritualization is effected not by becoming anti-matter or extra-matter, but by being drawn trans-Matter. Teilhard is the apostle of communion with God through the Earth.

Thus, the mystical theology of Teilhard is obviously not identical with that of John of the Cross (any more than the spirituality of St. Paul is identical with that of the Beloved Disciple). Yet, these two points of views are reconcilable. They do converge in their depths upon the same ineffable mystery of God's transforming love. Each contains its own personal contribution to Christian mysticism. Moreover, each complements the other within the vast theological and mystical pluralism of the Church. Nonetheless, there remains considerable difference of emphasis and tone between Teilhard and St. John of the Cross.

The movement of John is towards the transcendent, towards what Teilhard calls God-on-high *(Dieu-en-Haut)*. Except for a few notable passages at the beginning of the *Spiritual Canticle,* the positive role of creatures in our sanctification remains obscure. The historical perspective of God-up-ahead *(Dieu-en-Avant)*—in other words, the God of Evolution—never crossed his mind. Nonetheless, neither in his personal life nor in his writings does John scorn what Teilhard calls the Divine Milieu or Matter. Even though John stresses the transcendent and *nada,* the reality of a Diaphany is not foreign to our quest for our Spouse in and through creatures.

In comparing their respective spiritualities, we find that on the whole Teilhard contributes more to a better understanding of God's immanence, his presence within the World. In some respects, he situates and explains the ascetical dimension of the spiritual life more positively and constructively than does John. Nevertheless, no one can touch the Mystical Doctor in what pertains specifically to the mystical dimension of interior development. Furthermore, no one has ever penetrated more deeply and with such insight into the advanced stages of faith, night and transforming union than St. John of the Cross. Needless to say, these advanced stages constitute par excellence receptivity of a superior order.

Both Teilhard and John first lived all that they later wrote concerning receptivity. The spiritual theology of each derives from intense faith-experiences seeking understanding. Whether it is a question of the purgation sustained during the battle of Verdun (1916) or of the purification endured during nine months of physical and mental anguish in a Toledan dungeon (1578), the mystery experienced by each has the same Agent and the identical Goal: namely, the divine influence within each detaching him in darkest faith from all egocentrism so that he can be united in purest love to God. Reflecting on this mystery with a faith rooted in the Gospel and in the living tradition of the Church, Teilhard and John discern and express substantially the same doctrine of receptivity, yet with all the uniqueness of their individual personalities, gifts and vocations.

The quintessence of that doctrine on receptivity is this:

All that I am and all that I am called to become, I receive from God: my personhood, my individuality, my existence, my self, my gifts, my call to transforming union. I receive all this in the raw, in the rough, in such a way that the process of my personal sanctification is a gradual interior movement from the imperfect to the pluperfect, from immaturity to ultra-maturity, from scattered bits and pieces to actual union with God in himself. I am already in the process of transforming union. The progressive act itself of becoming more and more one with God transforms me into a state of perfection which is totally beyond my self or

133

my capabilities. Thus, everything which is accomplished in me in view of my transformation in God is done by God. I let it be done (Luke 1:38).

This élan, this becoming, this letting-it-be-done follows a general pattern.

First, aware of my self and of my gifts, I plunge into created things and there mingling with them elicit from my personhood and from them as rich a nature as I am capable of and as circumstances permit. I increase so that Christ may increase. This immersion into creation requires a very serious discipline, a veritable ascesis on my part. I perceive certain stops, immaturities, hang-ups, and do something positive to counteract them. This positive action is called mortification, active purification or simply common sense.

My ability to know myself and my real needs, however, is severely handicapped. The intricacies of my inner poverty and the depths of my personhood are so ineffable that beyond a certain relatively superficial point I cannot penetrate myself or anyone else. Here God must take a more directly active and interior role in my spiritualization. Indeed, he must take over entirely. Moreover, I cannot continue in the direction of immersion into creation indefinitely. The very effort of immersion requires an eventual emergence from all that is created. I must decrease so that Christ may further increase (John 3:30). This is the specifically Christian hour—and a grave one at that—but one full of inestimable peace and joy for the man or woman of faith and prayer. Here begins the specifically mystical movement. This threshold marks the beginning of contemplation, the passive night of sense and spirit.

From here on, there is no limit to what God can do in me (Eph. 3:20).

The mystery of receptivity can be epitomized thus: Whatever is effected in me in order to transform me is done by God, and

he accomplishes this in a complete kenosis of my entire being.
This is the ultimate in Christian receptivity: I let God be done in
me.

Sic finis libri, non autem mysterii.

Notes from Conclusion

1. *HM*, pp. 80–102.